12/03

RO400260816

Pages torn

DESTINATION
Chicago Jazz

SANDOR DEMLINGER AND JOHN STEINER

ARCADIA

First Published 2003
Reprinted 2003

Published in the United Kingdom by:
Tempus Publishing Ltd
The Mill, Brimscombe Port
Stroud, Gloucestershire GL5 2QG

Published in the United States of America by:
Arcadia Publishing
Charleston SC, Chicago, Portsmouth NH,
San Francisco

Library of Congress Catalog Card Number: 2003103135

Printed in Great Britain

For all general information contact Arcadia Publishing at:
Telephone 843-853-2070
Fax 843-853-0044
E-Mail sales@arcadiapublishing.com

For customer service and orders:
Toll-Free 1-888-313-2665

Visit us on the internet at http://www.arcadiapublishing.com

For more information on original photographs by Sandor Demlinger contact:
Sandor Demlinger
P.O. Box 3463
Fullerton, CA 92834-3463

DEDICATION

To Riva, my wonderful wife and mother of our children:

Keith Demlinger, Msc.D.; Glenn Demlinger, O.D.;

and Chef Allyson Demlinger

CONTENTS

State Street in 1921 was like a huge outdoor mall with shoppers everywhere. Aside from the Chicago, and the State and Lake Street Theaters, there was only one small vaudeville house near Randolph Street. (Demlinger Collection.)

ACKNOWLEDGMENTS

FIRST OF ALL, I cannot thank the great Dr. John Steiner enough. He inspired me to keep working to complete this book, even though he knew he could not see it finished. Together we traveled all over the city to document and photograph the places and people who were part of jazz music history. It was a safe bet that the old auto he drove wouldn't be stolen, no matter what neighborhood we were in, day or night. John was the kind of person that people knew on sight. A good example was a night we went calling on the Yanceys on the South Side. It was pitch dark and a man stood in our way until we approached him—then, "Oh, it's Mister Steiner, go on then."

A special thanks to Charles Sengstock, who knew John and the book we were working on well. His historic recollections were very important in the writing of this book and in music history in general. Thanks also for his photo of the 1111 Club on the North Side.

I am indebted to Nina Steiner, John's wife, who in her delicate way told me to finish the book and gave permission to use anything that John had given me for the book.

I would like to thank my loving wife, Reva, for her patience and understanding over the many years I have spent putting this book together.

Others who have aided in various ways with information and photographs to use in this book are as follows:

Merrit Jacobson: for photos of Don O'Neil's breakfast club jam session and the Apex Club jam session.

Ralph Williams: for his photos of the Edelweiss Gardens, early newspaper ads of the Frolics, the McVickers Theater stage photos, and other newspaper ads.

Duncan Schiedt: for photos of the jam session with Volly DeFaut and E. Murphy; Frankie Trumbaure and his orchestra; and the Sid Dawson band.

Frank Gillis: for his Muggsy Spanier studio portrait and photo of Jimmy McPartland.

William Russell and William Wagner: for 1930s photos of Chicago's South Side buildings, theaters, Mecca Flats, and street scenes, including the Grand Theater, Royal Gardens, Vendome Theater, Sunset and Grand Terrace Ballrooms.

Jean Bach: for help in identifying photos and historic information.

Ward Silver: for a series of photos taken at John Steiner's jam session at his home and other photos.

Mr. and Mrs. Richard Mushlitz: for photos of jam sessions and help in identifying people in photos.

Doc Cenard: for photos of 1949 jam session with Doc Evans, Al Jenkins, et. al.

The Historic New Orleans Collection: for photos of Jelly Roll Morton and Tony Jackson.

Charles Walton: for the photo of the Savoy Ballroom, information concerning the local union problems and related information on black and white musician union policies, and the story about the DuSable Hotel.

Don Erman: for his photo of the jam with Baby Dodds, Bud Freeman, and Muggsy Spanier.

Bob Lovelt: for the photo of young jazz players sitting in with Lee Collins.

S.W. Bowerman: for the photos of the jam session at 2 East Bank Street.

James Dapogny: for the input and information he gave John Steiner.

Bette Andre: for the photo of Junie Cobb Annabelle.

David Phillips: for the use of the Kaufmann & Fabry photos.

Bob Doss: a world-class artist who drew the maps for this book.

Special thanks to Ted Mesmer for his lists of jazz fans and clubs.

Thanks to Chuck Sullivan for the photo of the White City bandstand.

Thanks to T.C. Mesmer and Frank Driggs.

Thanks to Mike Spiegel and Samantha "Lulu" Gleisten of Arcadia Publishing.

Special thanks to Deborah Gillaspie of the Chicago Jazz Archive, University of Chicago Library.

And thanks to any other photographers, writers, or musicians who may have contributed to this book through their relationship with John Steiner.

INTRODUCTION

IN WRITING ABOUT JAZZ MUSIC, there is no point more important to make than the story of Chicago's place in its history. This book chronicles, in photographs, jazz music as it pertains to this great city.

Chicago and its music scene are constantly changing. Flash back to the 1940s and 50s and we can see some of the possible reasons. When World War II ended, much of the luster of bars, saloons, and nightclubs was wearing off. The veterans of the war had returned; there were no more weekend passes for new recruits. The nightclubs that hosted live music were hit hard. Jazz combos were replaced by recordings, and along South State Street buildings and theaters fell to the wrecking ball. In place of jazz halls stood entire blocks of empty lots. Even downtown Chicago was feeling the crunch, and most of the theaters were slowly being torn down. For example, only the historic Chicago Theater now remains on State Street.

But before people began leaving the downtown shopping district for the outlying neighborhood malls, Chicago was a busy, bustling place. There were several very fine photography studios headquartered downtown, some dating back to the early 1890s. Chicago's commercial photography studios did business with manufacturers in the city and in its suburbs. Chicago was the center of the catalog business with Sears and Roebuck, Spiegel, and Montgomery Ward—to name just a few. Each studio got its share. But there was also another side to photographing the city. Real estate agents had a need for photos of their buildings in order to rent or sell. City planners needed photos of entire streets. It was logical for photographers to be employed by dozens of offices.

In our quest for photographs of important places that had been known to harbor jazz bands, jazz entertainers, and music makers we searched high and low for pictures. Unfortunately, aside from some movie theaters, the places we wanted to show had not been photographed by any of the major studios. Only Kaufmann and Fabry, where I had worked, came to our rescue.

Years later, one of the salesmen, Dave Kleinman, purchased Kaufmann's. I went to Kleinman and asked if I could go over the glass

negatives that had once belonged to Kaufmann. He warned me to hurry up the stairs as his clerk, "Old Lady Garvey," was making room and trashing the plates right then and there. After I spent a good hour there and carried a large handful of negatives out, I thanked Dave Kleinman very much. His parting words to me were, "Sandy, you can use them for the jazz book, but I don't want to see them hanging all over the city." No Dave, I haven't hung them all over Chicago, and yes, 45 years later they are going to appear in the jazz book.

There were other sources of jazz music history in the city, the South Side's *Chicago Defender* newspaper was incredibly significant and contained a lot of important news. Tragically, a fire in the building destroyed their entire photo file. *Down Beat* magazine did a lot to tell the story of Chicago's jazz and music scene, as well as the earlier *Metronome* magazine. But most of these photos were unobtainable.

As we study these photographs, we realize how precious they are, simply because they were made on thin paper and could be crumpled, ripped, or cracked very easily. They could also have been tossed out, as in the case of Daguerre, the South Side photographer whose niece had no room for his boxes of glass negatives that no one wanted and so she had to throw them out. Mr. Daguerre's photographs of King Oliver's Jazz Band, Louis Armstrong, and many other New Orleans greats were probably on those plate negatives.

We are very fortunate indeed to have been given Bill Russell's prints of photos he took in the 1930s of the Royal Gardens, the Cabin Inn, Warwick Hall, the Grand Theater, and several other places of historic importance. Even the photographs taken by John and I are of places that are no longer standing. Apartment buildings came to replace entire blocks of jazz joints on North Wells Street.

When I talked with John at his home in Milwaukee he would tell me about movie theaters and buildings we had photographed—places that were no longer standing. "You mean they tore down the Regal Theater?" I asked him one day. And they had.

A lot has been written about jazz music and Chicago's place in its history. But I would like to pay homage to Chicago's extended family of photographers. Many have taken historic jazz photographs, but they are all part of the city's early photography history, when only the small studios played a part in documenting the places and people who lived there. Knowing that photographers had to scratch out a living at this art form, they would have accepted any kind of assignment.

The following is a list of the studios I have been able to locate and find samples of their work.

The Howe Studios, South Paulina Street
Mosher's Historical National Photo Art, 951 Wabash Avenue
Bell Studios, 96 State Street
Rocher Studios, 702 State Street
Hulfren Studios, 2029 Wabash Avenue
Kanberg Studios, 433 East Division Street
Brands Photo Studio, 210 Wabash Avenue
George Riel Photography, 339 West Madison Street
Harris Studios, 150 State Street
George J. Klein Practical Photography, 206 North Clark Street
J.E.Waters, 414 East 63rd Street
Wilson Photography, 389 State Street
Wilke Studios, 393 Blue Island Avenue
Stevens Art Studios in the McVickers Theatre Building
Max Platz Studios, 88 North Clark Street
H. Rocher, 724 Wabash Avenue
Smith's Studios, 206 North Clark Street (awarded at the Paris Expo of 1878)
Bloom Studios, Downtown
Heidrich Blessing, Near North
Lawrence Studios- Downtown
Kaufmann and Fabry, South Wabash Avenue
Shigeta Wright Studio, North Wells Street
Daguerre Studios, South Side

The Stock Yard Inn was a home away from home for cattle and beef buyers, as Chicago was the meat packing capital of the United States for a long period. On Chicago's South Side, cattle were shipped in from all the states, processed, and sent out. Entertaining the cattle moguls, the inn had some of the finest dining and dancing in the city. Many types of music were offered here, including hot jazz bands and sweet music for listening. (Demlinger Collection.)

CHAPTER ONE

Chicago Jazz

CHICAGO! It was a "Stomp off, let's go!" kind-of-town, according to the title of the Fletcher Henderson tune on an early Columbia record.

The fact that Chicago was the railroad center of the United States may have sped up the migration of southern musicians eager to leave New Orleans and find work in the north. The New Orleans musicians who could muster the cash made the trip, while others scrambled for jobs on riverboats heading up the Mississippi and then made their way to Chicago. In 1917, the U.S. Navy closed down most of the places in the Storyville district of New Orleans, an area famous for its Dixieland Jazz and swinging night life. With World War I going on in Europe, the Navy frowned upon the fact that off-duty sailors could be distracted by all the excitement and vice that the saloons, bars, and theaters of this red light district provided. So the musicians headed north.

Many New Orleans musicians got the message that Chicago, Illinois, was a city with opportunities waiting to be had. Word had already been filtering down south that there were hundreds of jobs for musicians up north, particularly in Chicago. The Windy City also offered many jobs in an assortment of different fields. The Chicago Union Stock Yards brought cattle from many western states to Chicago, and jobs were plentiful at the many meat packing factories in the city. Giant steel mills outside of Gary, Indiana, provided further opportunities. Chicago was also the center of the Midwest's grain and feed business, and had a free-wheeling mayor who kept the new businesses coming. And a developing black community was beginning to make its mark in Chicago music history.

Chicago made a home for many new residents and the music they brought with them, in the South Side, Downtown, and Near North Side neighborhoods. The North Side of the city was still developing and the West Side was still busy finding its musical place by doing the polka, two-step, and waltz. Musicians migrating from the south would arrive in Chicago at either Twelfth Street or Union Station, and they did not have far to walk to find work. Their welcoming committee was led by Jelly Roll Morton and Tony Jackson, who were already busy working. Morton had been performing at the Pekin Theater since 1910. Jackson was at the Elite Number One, which was

also on South State Street. They would quickly find the newly arriving musicians places to live, either at rooming houses or at lodges, such as The Mecca Flats, which was located at 3338–3360 South State Street, now part of the Illinois Institute of Technology campus.

By 1913, the original Creole Jazz Band was playing at the Grand Theater, breaking it up between vaudeville acts, singers, and comics. Even dog and pony acts would be on the bill and the music would play along with them. In 1914, the first white band to come north and play hot New Orleans-style music was Tom Brown's Ragtime Band. They appeared at Lamb's Cafe in downtown Chicago despite objections voiced by a local musician's union. According to legend, the term "jass," which was vaguely slang for sex and associated with prostitution, was used to denigrate the band and the club. Lamb's Cafe was using non-union workers and union employees picketing outside used the term "jass music." The plan backfired, however, and only made the band, and their style of music, increasingly popular. Tom Brown and Lamb's owners picked up on the word and advertised that Tom Brown's Jass Band was now playing. The word got out and people began calling it "jazz" and packing the place nightly just to hear what hot jazz sounded like.

In 1914, some of the best musicians from New Orleans were arriving in Chicago eager to work. Another white band called the Louisiana Five got it going fast and furious when they opened up at the Casino Gardens. Its members included Nick LaRocca on cornet, Anton Lada on drums, Yellow Nunes on clarinet, Eddie Edwards on trombone, and Harry Ragas at the piano. They led the way for all the great black bands that would be coming north. When Anton Lada looked inside the Casino, he muttered, "I thought we had dives in New Orleans but this place had anything we had beat by a mile. There wasn't room in there to take a leak."

When Joe "King" Oliver came north in 1918, it marked the beginning of the greatest hot jazz music to be played and heard anywhere in the world. Joe Oliver was so popular that he had to play in two bands, going from Bill Johnson's band at the Dreamland to the Royal Gardens where Jimmie Noone had his band tearing the roof down. Oliver was so busy playing all over that he finally called upon many of his New Orleans buddies and

Above: The El tracks above 63rd Street bisect Drexel Avenue and on this corner, looming high on the rooftop, reads a sign for the building's dancehall. El riders also saw a sign reading DANCING at the street level entrance doorway. (Demlinger Photograph.)

formed his own band, calling it King Oliver's Creole Jazz Band. The band members were Johnny Dodds on clarinet, Baby Dodds on drums, Lil Hardin on piano, Honore Dutrey on trombone, and Ed Garland on bass.

Oliver's band played at the Dreamland Ballroom for the first few years, but when they moved to the Lincoln Gardens, Joe Oliver sensed his band needed a lift. So he called upon a youngster named Louis Armstrong who he heard a few times before he left New Orleans. Armstrong would play second cornet behind him. The early electric recordings of the band by the Okeh label hardly do them justice.

With the open door policy on the South Side of town and the lack of hot music being played there before the migration, it was prime territory for musical expansion. As the large influx of musicians headed into Chicago's South Side, the area began catering to the many people who wanted to escape the more typical music happening in other areas of the city. When the Casino Gardens opened, its orchestra featured Eddie Edwards on trombone and Harry Ragas on piano. Catering to upper-class whites, the Casino Gardens would hire only the top bands to perform there.

Chicago became the new home to two of the greatest jazz legends to migrate from New Orleans. The first was Jelly Roll Morton, who among other things claimed to have "invented jazz music," according to the August 1938 issue of *Down Beat* magazine. Morton was a creative genius who wrote amazing music. In the hands of his band, the Red Hot Peppers, his music was played with so much gusto and excitement that even today it raises the bar a little higher for jazz musicians. Morton's songs, such as "The Pearls," "King Porter Stomp," "Kansas City Stomp," and "The Wolverine Blues," are but a few examples of his important contributions. When he was asked about "The King Porter Stomp," he explained that he just made up the name. "The Kansas City Stomp" was named for a bar in Tijuana, Mexico. In *Mr. Jelly Roll*, Jelly Roll tells Alan Lomax about his experiences in the New Orleans Red Light District as a child, and staying out until 11:00 p.m. on Saturdays and Sundays.

"So I went with some other kids to the Tenderloin District, which was the Red Light District of New Orleans. One time we heard that one of the sporting houses was stuck for a pianist. So my pals talked me into going for the job. I was so scared I told them I wouldn't go unless they went too. So the owner, upon seeing all of us, placed us in a room out of sight to the other guests. I began to play, and all of a sudden, people were tipping me to keep playing. The owners wanted to give me the job right away, but I said no. Afraid my folks would find out since they didn't want me near the district at all. When I asked what the salary would be the landlady said she would pay $1 a night, but you would make a lot in tips."

All the girls liked Jelly Roll and worked on their customers to tip him. Morton made more money than he had ever seen. Bunk Johnson commented that, "Jelly played in only white houses in those days, only him and Tony Jackson, the other musicians couldn't play there."

Morton moved north to Chicago and settled in, playing and cutting solo and band records. Many jazz aficionados have agreed that he is one of the greatest jazz immortals of all times.

The other early important jazz musician to migrate north was Tony Jackson. Jackson, a genius singer and piano player, went on to join the Original Creole Band when enough musicians arrived in town. According to Morton, Tony Jackson was the world's greatest single-handed entertainer of all time. Jackson was a favorite New Orleans pianist because he would play any tune, any opera, and sing along with the music. When he came to Chicago he was an instant success as he sat in with Freddie Keppard's band at the Pekin and Grand Theaters. In addition, he would play solo at several bars and clubs late in the evening. Jackson began drinking heavily, leading to his eventual decline and early death. John St. Cyr, a famous New Orleans banjo player and guitarist, said it all when he proclaimed that Jelly Roll was great, but Tony Jackson was the best there was. Even pianist composer Clarence Williams believed that Jackson was the greatest Blues pianist to ever live, because of his ability to lace original ideas with impeccable melody. "Everybody just copied him, including myself," said Williams.

Tony Jackson faced a difficult plight. Aside from the racism he faced as an African American, he was afflicted with epilepsy and later in life became an alcoholic. He was reportedly a very sensitive man and his music may have helped him cope. Jackson, it was said, wrote a lot of music and would sell the manuscripts for a few dollars. People would then buy the original music and publish it as their own, making much more than they paid Jackson. Unfortunately, there are no known recordings of his playing.

THE BLUES

The history of Chicago jazz inevitably includes the city's great blues musicians. Their recordings, listed as "race records," appeared on several labels, including Paramount, Okeh, Columbia, Black Swan, Brunswick, and Perfect. Black Patti, Crown Labels, and the Gennett Company in Indiana produced some of the rarest albums. Most are long forgotten, but many Chicago blues artists live on through their recordings. The work of Bessie Smith, Blind Lemon Jefferson, Ma Rainey, Blind Blake, and Ida Cox, to name just a few, greatly influenced and helped to shape the jazz music it preceded.

Chicago's famous Mecca Flats housed many an early jazzmen and had rooms to spare when the migrating New Orleans musicians came to Chicago. The Flats was home to many for as long as they wanted it to be and as long as they paid the rent. It was also the subject of Jimmie Blythe and Alexander Robinson's song, "Mecca Flat Blues," which was similar to other blues melodies, and the words fit the bill. The song starts out, "Talk about blues/ I've got the meanest kind, blues/ and disgusted, dissatisfied in mind. My Mecca Flat man, he just don't understand."

At this busy Chicago intersection in 1915, Canal Street depicts a scene similar to that found in many urban areas of the time. Look closely in the window of the corner bar to see a white-clothed bartender watching the photographer. (Demlinger Collection.)

CHAPTER TWO

South State Street

1910–1930s

WHEN JAZZ CAME TO CHICAGO, it entered through South State Street. In the early 1910s, jazz music could be heard coming from the stage of the Grand Theater on South State Street. By the early 1920s, every club, lounge, bar, and theater had a jazz band. The many theaters on South State Street all had pit bands, bands on balconies, or on stage. The many musicians needed for this amount of work was overwhelming, so many musicians went from job to job working all night. Sometimes theater concerts would actually end up as battles of the bands, each trying to outdo the other. The Vendome Theater at 3143 South State Street was one such venue, at times featuring Freddie Keppard and Sidney Bechet blasting away at Joe "King" Oliver and his band who were across the street at the Grand Theater.

At the corner of State and 27th Street was the Pekin Theater, which always had fine vaudeville acts to go along with the stage plays they would put on. The Pekin really made elaborate stage productions with large casts of characters that provided not only entertainment, but medical care as well. During the hot Chicago summer months the theater's few large skylights didn't allow too much air movement. So, just in case, a doctor was always on hand for weary patrons. The Pekin lasted into the 1930s and then became a South Side police station for several more years.

The Savoy Bar is where Tony Jackson hung his hat. The great triple threat entertainer was said to be, by most New Orleans' musicians, the best piano player that ever lived. The first New Orleans musician to arrive in Chicago, he had been chased out of his hometown because of his effeminate ways. Tony Jackson was known to compose his songs in minutes. Many lesser musicians would steal his tunes and claim them as their own. At age 15, he was playing at the most expensive saloons in New Orleans. Playing, dancing, and even singing opera melodies.

Much like Jackson, Jelly Roll Morton was next in line as the best piano player in town. He too arrived in Chicago very early and instantly obtained a job playing piano at the Pekin Theater. Morton also was a music writer and composed many compositions for his soon-to-be jazz band. Among his important compositions are "The King Porter Stomp," "The Pearls," "Wolverine Blues," and "Sidewalk Blues." Morton's Red Hot Pepper band on Victor Records produced some of the best Morton material. His band had at one time or another George Mitchell or Lee Collins on trumpet, Kid Ory on trombone, and many other great New Orleans musicians. Lee Collins said that Morton stole his tune for "Sidewalk Blues," but who's to argue.

There are many lasting memories of Jelly Roll Morton as he recorded many sides for the Library of Congress, playing examples of various artists and how they would play certain tunes, along with examples of his own songs. In addition, Bill Russell has written a large volume about Morton, published by the Historic New Orleans Collection.

On State Street, beside the theaters and bars, was the famous Mecca Flats apartment building. This huge complex at one time had a park-like interior with gardens and flowers growing so that apartment dwellers could look out of their windows to the lovely scene below. When Bill Russell took a photo of it in 1930, it was a just a big apartment building with stores on State Street that included a tailor shop, a general merchandise store, and a community center. In the 1920s, a few doors away stood Clarence Williams' Music Publishers. This was where a musician would bring a melody and Williams would write out the score and publish it for them for a fee. The original writer would only get a few pennies for the song even if it got recorded, as that was the way in those days.

Louis Armstrong's recording of "The Oriental Strut" must have been named after the café by that name, which was a mere stone's throw from where he was playing. Musicians often got the names of their songs from places where they were playing. Another example of this would be Jimmie

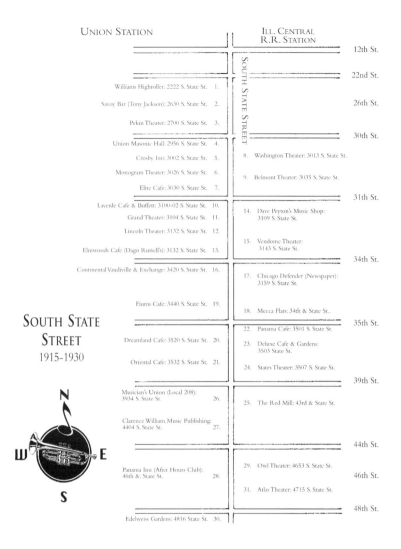

UNION STATION

ILL. CENTRAL
R.R. STATION

12th St.

22nd St.

SOUTH STATE STREET

26th St.

Williams Highroller: 2222 S. State St.   1.

Savoy Bar (Tony Jackson): 2630 S. State St.   2.

Pekin Theater: 2700 S. State St.   3.

30th St.

Union Masonic Hall: 2956 S. State St.   4.

Crosby Inn: 3002 S. State St.   5.   8.   Washington Theater: 3013 S. State St.

Monogram Theater: 3026 S. State St.   6.   9.   Belmont Theater: 3035 S. State St.

Elite Cafe: 3030 S. State St.   7.

31st St.

Laverde Cafe & Buffett: 3100-02 S. State St.   10.   14.   Dave Peyton's Music Shop:
                                                              3109 S. State St.

Grand Theater: 3104 S. State St.   11.

Lincoln Theater: 3132 S. State St.   12.   15.   Vendome Theater:
                                                    3143 S. State St.

Elmwoods Cafe (Dago Russell's): 3132 S. State St.   13.

34th St.

Continental Vaudiville & Exchange: 3420 S. State St.   16.   17.   Chicago Defender (Newspaper):
                                                                     3159 S. State St.

                                                               18.   Mecca Flats: 34th & State St..

Fiums Cafe: 3440 S. State St.   19.

**SOUTH STATE
STREET**
1915-1930

35th St.

                                                    22.   Panama Cafe: 3501 S. State St.

Dreamland Cafe: 3520 S. State St.   20.   23.   Deluxe Cafe & Gardens:
                                                  3503 State St.

Oriental Cafe: 3532 S. State St.   21.   24.   States Theater: 3507 S. State St.

39th St.

Musician's Union (Local 208):
3934 S. State St.   26.   25.   The Red Mill: 43rd & State St.

Clarence William Music Publishing:
4404 S. State St.   27.

44th St.

Panama Inn (After Hours Club):
46th & State St.   28.   29.   Owl Theater: 4653 S. State St.

                            31.   Atlas Theater: 4715 S. State St.

46th St.

48th St.

Edelweiss Gardens: 4816 State St.   30.

N
W   E
S

Noone's "Apex Club Blues," named for a nightclub where he and his band played. The famous "Royal Garden Blues" got its name from the Royal Gardens, after its name was changed from the Lincoln Gardens.

There was an exciting atmosphere for outside dancing at many of the early dance halls and ballrooms. Chicago's hot summers made it quite important for the owners of these places to provide an area for dancing couples to be more comfortable. They would hang oriental lamps around

the edges of the dance floor providing wonderful decoration and color. Among the ballrooms doing this were the Edelweiss Gardens and Williams High Roller. Most often the small clubs that opened along South State Street were nothing but stores turned into bars and saloons or lunch counters. But they were places to play music and the customers loved it.

One important jazz establishment was the Dreamland Café, later called the Cabin Inn. It catered to a high class of people because they not only had the best bands but also served fine food and alcohol. It may have been a gangster get-away as well. But back in 1918, the finest New Orleans musicians played at the Dreamland Café. One headliner was Doc Cook's Dreamland Ballroom Orchestra, which broke all records for turnouts. During its long tenure at the Dreamland, Cook's Orchestra didn't make many personnel changes. The main ensemble was made up of Bert Green, Fred Garland, Andrew Hillaire, Freddie Keppard, Jimmie Noone, and John St Cyr. Many of these musicians would also record with Armstrong with his "Hot Five" or "Hot Seven" jazz sides on the Okeh label. King Oliver's band also played at the Dreamland and while he was there, Muggsy Spanier managed to sneak in, since he knew the doorman. Muggsy would climb up into the balcony where the band would be playing just to listen to Oliver's solos and the band's songs. As soon as he heard King Oliver, he was hooked.

It was during his time at the Dreamland that Oliver sent for Armstrong to join him in Chicago. After Oliver left in 1923, it was the Ollie Power's orchestra, featuring Glover Compton on piano, that provided all the music for the Dreamland dancers.

A jazzy place for dancers was the Dusty Bottom, named because the floor had straw sprinkled all over it. The corner of State and 35th Streets had a number of historical jazz places. The States Theater, although small, still put on live shows and had jazz bands that filled the seats every night. Two doors west was a three-story building and up one flight was the Apex Club 10, where Jimmie Noone and his jazz band played on and on. The band consisted of Baby Dodds, Earl Hines, George Mitchell, and a few pick-up musicians. Most of this band recorded with Jelly Roll Morton's Red Hot Peppers and Armstrong's Hot Five.

Down near the end of South State Street's jazz strut area, the Edelweiss Gardens held fort. In 1920, the great Ted Lewis had a hot band there and he would feature some of jazz history's greatest musicians. The Edelweiss Gardens had one of the finest outdoor ballrooms. There was always either a jazz band playing or a vaudeville act performing.

Over at the Sunset, when he wasn't playing elsewhere in some other band, Louis Armstrong brought down the house. At the Grand Terrace Ballroom, Earl Hines' orchestra stayed for many months with a great lineup of talent including Rex Stewart on trumpet. Tommy Ladiner and Jimmie Noone would also sit in between their own club jobs.

On the corner of State and 27th Street stood the famous Pekin Theater, which featured vaudeville acts and music concerts as early as 1910. Jelly Roll Morton played piano here soon after arriving in town around 1915. He would play his own brand of piano in between acts and convinced many New Orleans musicians to join him there.

In 1920, King Oliver's Creole Jazz Band was playing at the Pekin with a terrific lineup. Many others took their turn playing the Pekin Theatre. Not only was it a good daily job, but upstairs there was the Beau Arts Café, a private and exclusive club.

In this early photograph, the Pekin was featuring a dog and pony show along with 10 other acts. Next door was the "Pekin Inn Café," later home to the Pekin Grand Photographic Studio where families came for formal portraits.

The Pekin Theatre later closed down and in the 1930s, it was converted into a South Side police station.

(Immediate) This rare photograph of pianist Tony Jackson shows him sitting at the piano. He was allegedly the first New Orleans musician to arrive in Chicago. To many who had the opportunity to hear him, Jackson was one of the greatest pianists to live. He created his own original style, which was copied by everyone. His influence is resounding and not only in relation to jazz and blues. Jackson was known to compose his songs in minutes. He was playing at the best saloons in New Orleans at the age of 15, and not only playing the piano but also dancing around while still hitting the keys and singing. (Photo courtesy of the Historic New Orleans Collection.)

This photograph shows Jelly Roll Morton at the piano in a pose for the photographer (possibly Bill Russell). Jelly Roll is believed to have been next in the line of New Orleans musicians to arrive in Chicago in the early 1900s. (Photo courtesy of the Historic New Orleans Collection.)

Ollie Power's fine orchestra poses for this photograph at the well-known Vendome Theater. Glover Compton is on piano. The table settings suggest that the Vendome of this period was more a supper club with dining and dancing than a movie house. Orchestras such as King Oliver's, Louis Armstrong's, and Freddie Keppard's would be on the stage entertaining. (Steiner Collection.)

The famous Vendome Theater, at 3145 South State at East 31st Street, was one of the hubs along South State Street at which many of the jazz orchestras and bands played. The Vendome, along with the Royal Gardens, the DeLuxe, the Sunset Café, and the Plantation Club, hosted "Battle of the Bands" competitions right into daylight hours and into the streets. "It was like New Orleans moved to Chicago," said Lee Collins.

Erskine Tate and the Vendome Orchestra would play at the Vendome and then run across the street to battle Freddie Keppard and King Oliver's band playing at the Plantation Club. Most of the acts made the rounds from theater to theater until after a few months they had finished the entire State Street circuit. It was a time when there weren't enough musicians to go around and performers had to move about to fill someone's shoes or replace a fellow in a band for a night or two.

In the mid-to late 1920s, Erskine Tate's orchestra sometimes featured Louis Armstrong playing duets with Fats Waller on organ. The band performed jazz concerts between movies. Tate's orchestra had a lineup that included, among others: Fayette Williams, James Tate, Jimmy Bertrand, Angelo Fernandez, Noval Morton, and Adrian Robinson. (From Bill Russell.)

The Mecca Flats, located at 3338–3360 South State Street, offered apartments and rooms to rent for reasonable rates. In those days, a place to flop after the long train or bus ride was all a musician could ask for. According to the Chicago Defender's *"Music News" page, there was a lot to do and much music to be heard in those flats. In this photograph by Bill Russell, shot in May 1950, one can only imagine the famous faces that stayed a night, a week, or even months at the Mecca Flats. Down the street was Clarence Williams' Music Publishers, where a musician who wrote songs could get them published—and likely recorded—while being paid for any music. (From Bill Russell.)*

Among the many early New Orleans arrivals in Chicago was drummer Paul Barbarin who left the Crescent City in 1917 and found work in Chicago's Armour and Company Stockyards. As soon as he secured a job, he sent for Buddy Petit, the fine trumpet player, but Petit refused to come north, and Joe Oliver and Jimmie Noone came instead. They soon opened at the Royal Gardens Café, located at 459 East 31st Street.

In 1919, Clarence and Spencer Williams, both from New Orleans though not related, composed "Royal Garden Blues" in honor of the South Side legendary dancehall.

When King Oliver opened at the Royal Gardens, his band consisted of Lee Collins on second trumpet, George Filhe on trombone, Junie Cobb on clarinet, Lil Hardin on piano, Stomp Evans on alto, Bud Scott on guitar, Bert Cobb on bass, and Clifford "Snags" Jones on the drums.

This photograph shows the Cabin Inn at 3520 South State Street in the 1930s. The Cabin Inn billed itself as one of the oddest nightclubs in town. The club allowed homosexuals, interracial dancing, and even had a transvestite chorus.

Back in 1918, the Cabin Inn was the Dreamland Café. Headlines would read: "Doc Cook's Dreamland Ballroom's Orchestra Breaks Records at the Dreamland." Cook enjoyed a long stay at the Dreamland and his lineup of stars didn't change daily. His ensemble included Bert Green, Fred Garland, Andrew Hilaire, Freddie Keppard, Jimmie Noone, and John St. Cyr. Keppard, Noone, Garland, and John St. Cyr were stand-out musicians who recorded with Armstrong on many of his Hot Five and Hot Seven Okeh recordings.

Even Oliver's orchestra played at the Dreamland, and while he was there, Muggsy Spanier (who lived on Chicago's West Side) managed to sneak in, since he knew the manager who allowed him to hide in the balcony and listen. Muggsy would go back home and tell all his buddies about the great sounds he heard. When Oliver called for Louis Armstrong to join him, Louis turned the place into a royal battle. Ollie Power's orchestra followed Oliver's band into the Dreamland with his Harmony Syncopators, who featured Glover Compton on piano in 1923. (Bill Russell Photograph.)

Several buildings were still standing on the corner of State and 35th Streets when John Steiner took this photograph in 1965. On the far right is the States Theater and to the left, on the second floor, is the famous Apex Club, located at 330 East 35th Street. There, Jimmie Noone and his Apex Club Jazz Band played from 1928 to 1930, at times featuring Bud Scott on guitar, Junie Cobb on banjo, Earl Hines on piano, and George Mitchell on trumpet. Mitchell also recorded with Jelly Roll Morton and his Red Hot Peppers. (Steiner Collection.)

e the band in the rear consisting of a cornet, flute, tuba, sax, and piano. Nellie Lewis, who
immediate foreground dancing with a man named Pet Baby. (Demlinger Collection.)

This very early portrait of Louis Armstrong shows him taking a break after doing a set. He holds his ever-present handkerchief he used to wipe his head and face. (Steiner Collection.)

This c. 1930s photograph taken by Bill Russell is the only known photograph of the Royal Gardens. Later known as the Lincoln Gardens, it is seen here locked up and for sale. Almost all the New Orleans orchestras played at the Gardens from time to time. In 1921, it became the Lincoln Gardens and in the early 1920s, King Oliver's Creole Jazz Band played there with Lil Hardin on piano, Louis Armstrong on cornet, Baby Dodds on drums, Johnny St. Cyr on banjo/guitar, and Stump Evans on alto sax.

The Gardens, like several other clubs, had an upstairs balcony where the band played to leave the entire dance floor open for guests. One Christmas Eve, a fire started and there was a stampede to get out. Lee Collins recalled, "Everyone grabbed a coat off the racks and I ended up with a real warm fur coat that sure was better than the paper one I came in with, and facing that Chicago cold, I was very happy to get it." (Steiner Collection.)

This photograph shows a string of land west of the 12th Street Railroad Station. Louis Armstrong and most of the other New Orleans musicians arriving on trains from the south would have seen this view when they arrived in Chicago. Note the small White City sign in the center of this photo. (Demlinger Collection.)

Richard M. Jones was leader and pianist of many fine jazz bands of the 1920s and 1930s. He hired the finest musicians available and drew on them to play on his record dates, in addition to his club shows. (Steiner Collection.)

The one and only Meade "Lux" Lewis sits at his piano in his apartment. (Steiner Collection.)

Glover Compton played piano with many of the leading South Side orchestras and musicians including Powers, Oliver, and Keppard. (Steiner Collection.)

Baby Dodds, the famous New Orleans drummer, enjoys a relaxing moment, still holding his drumsticks as he talks. Dodds was the drummer on many recordings, including King Oliver's and many New Orleans bands that recorded in Chicago. (Steiner Collection.)

The three performers who mug for the camera, from left to right, are Dol Jones, Byron (?), and Alice Calloway. (Steiner Collection.)

South Dearborn Street looked like this in the early 1930s. Jimmy Yancey's house was the fourth from the left, according to Bill Russell, who took this photograph. (Steiner Collection.)

The Chicago Defender's Saturday edition in February 1930 describes bookings around the country. This edition included bookings of Chicago's own Butterbeans and Suzy in Cleveland, Ohio. It also ran an illustrated ad for the Grand Theater and its "Brown Skin Models in Paris" review. (Steiner Collection.)

These tickets to the Grand Theater were what John Steiner was able to pick up after the wrecking crew finished tearing it down. One can almost name the year of issue by the prices: 11¢ to 14¢ to 20¢ to 35¢. During the war years of the 1940s, many movie houses charged 11¢. (Steiner Collection.)

The Grand Theater at 3110–12 South State Street was one of the first places to host jazz music in Chicago. Along with the usual stage and variety shows, the Grand offered music at intermission featuring the best available orchestras. These c. 1930s photographs, above and at left, show the famous King Kong on the bill for 10¢. (Both photos by Bill Russell.)

Mister Butterbeans, of the famous novelty act of Butterbeans and Suzy, greeted John Steiner on his front steps. Suzy was too ill to come out, and he was sorry for that. Their house used to belong to Lovey Austin, the famous blues singer. The Okeh recording company made several records of them singing, and even Louis Armstrong recorded with them. (Demlinger Photograph.)

These rare studio photographs of Chicago performers who played at the Pekin and Grand Theaters were probably taken between 1910 and 1915 and possibly earlier. The Bloom Studio was one of the studios in Chicago that took photographs of stage and musical performers. (Demlinger Collection.)

This rare 1920 view of Ted Lewis inside the Edelweiss Gardens was a gift from Ralph Williams to John Steiner. Ted Lewis signed it to "Nig Williams." (Steiner Collection.)

In small clubs or large dancehalls, Earl "Fatha" Hines was equally at home. Hines played a lot around Chicago, mostly with Jimmie Noone at the Apex Club or his own band at the Grand Terrace Ballroom. He surrounded himself with top musicians such as Charlie Parker, Louis Armstrong, and Dizzy Gillespie. (Steiner Collection.)

This early photograph of King Oliver's Dixie Syncopators by Daguerre was made at the Plantation Café, 338 East 35th Street. Members of his band at this time included a young Barney Bigard on sax and clarinet, Paul Barbarin on drums, and Arthur "Bud" Scott on banjo. (Steiner Collection.)

The three jazz musicians pictured at a gathering at Junie Cobb's house are, from left to right, Roy Palmer, Jasper Taylor, and Junie Cobb (seated). (Steiner Collection.)

Above: John H. Wickliffe's famous Ginger Band played for dancers at the Entertainer Café at 35th and Indiana Avenue, and the DeLuxe Gardens at 3503 State Street. This small advertisement suggests a visit when on "The Stroll." (Steiner Collection.)

At left: The Yo-Yo Blues, sung by Blind Lemon Jefferson, was a popular recording published on the Paramount label. (Steiner Collection.)

The Livery Stable Blues was one of the earliest jazz songs written with the word "Blues" in it. Played by the Original Dixieland Jazz Band, it was made famous by Muggsy Spanier and George Brunies on the Bluebird recording series. (Steiner Collection.)

At right: This rare Race Record jacket features Mama and Jimmy Yancey in the center. (Steiner Collection.)

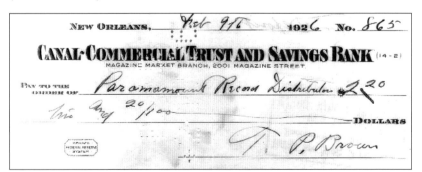

The Paramount Record Company received this check for the sum of $2.20 in 1926 from T.P. Brown. (Demlinger Collection.)

CHAPTER THREE
South Side

1900–1965

MANY would argue that jazz history in Chicago begins on the city's South Side with the events that laid the foundation for the Great Migration and the arrival and success of so many jazz musicians.

Turn-of-the-century Chicago saw rapid growth as industry and economics established the city as a major commercial center. The area's stockyards, steel plants, and railroads brought jobs and opportunity, but they also brought money and the potential for vice and corruption. Chicago, "city of big shoulders" and "hog butcher to the world" (in the words of Carl Sandburg), was equally renown for its "painted women," criminal ways, and corrupt politicians. The Windy City was a major outpost for organized crime, and local politicians and officials were known for looking the other way and opening their pockets. It was, after all, a "wide-open town."

One Chicago area infamous for the crime, vice, gambling, and prostitution was the Custom House Levee District, one of the most renowned historic red-light districts in the world. The area, bounded by Dearborn Street on the east, Clark Street on the west, Polk Street on the south, and Harrison Street on the north, contained 33 brothels, 36 saloons, 9 lodging houses, and 10 pawn brokers. Women could be seen encouraging would-be customers to enter a given house of ill-repute for an affair to remember. Often, depending on the reputation of the brothel, men and boys would leave robbed and beaten, with little but their undershirts.

Mary Hastings ran a series of well-known brothels. Hastings opened her place near Harrison and Polk after first obtaining a license to do so. Soon she was running four houses and all were making money. Rumor has it that Mary Hastings often said that her harlots had been thrown out of "decent houses," and that if a girl was good enough to get into one of the first-class parlor houses, she would be too good for her place.

Of all the lavish clubs and whorehouses in the city, none could compare to the one that the Everleigh sisters had built. Each parlor was given a different name and decorated with lavish trim. The Gold, Moorish, Silver, Copper, Rose, Green, Blue, Oriental, Chinese, Egyptian, and Japanese rooms were all decorated and furnished to fit the name. Even the music being played for customers had to fit the design of the room.

According to legend, a no-smoking reformer would come into the house regularly to preach to anyone who would listen to her. On one occasion, as she was handing out anti-tobacco leaflets, she rushed into the kitchen where Minna Everleigh was going over the day's menu with the chief chef. She screamed, "Minna! Your girls are going straight to hell! You must stop them."

"What can I do?" asked Minna.

"You, you can make them stop smoking cigarettes!"

There were several weekly newspapers that reported on the local goings-on in the Levee and red-light districts. A man named Shang Andrews reported short accounts about the girls working there or the drunks that some folks would know about. Tidbits of the accounts would go something like this:

"Lulu Lee, a local streetwalker, has gone into a home to reform herself, but we think it will fail."

"The Dive on North LaSalle Street called A Wine Hall is owned by an old procuress. Most any night that you go there you'll find young boys, prostitutes, thieves, and 'Vags.'"

"We are happy to inform the public that old-timer Frankie Warner has left the city."

This area, which was slowly becoming home to a growing African-American population, soon welcomed the traveling New Orleans musicians who found their place to play and live not far from the red lights. When Jelly Roll Morton and Tony Jackson arrived in Chicago in 1910, the Windy City was ripe with scandalous entertainment, organized crime, and gambling. And the stage was set for the influential music these New Orleans musicians brought with them.

SOUTH SIDE 1920–1965

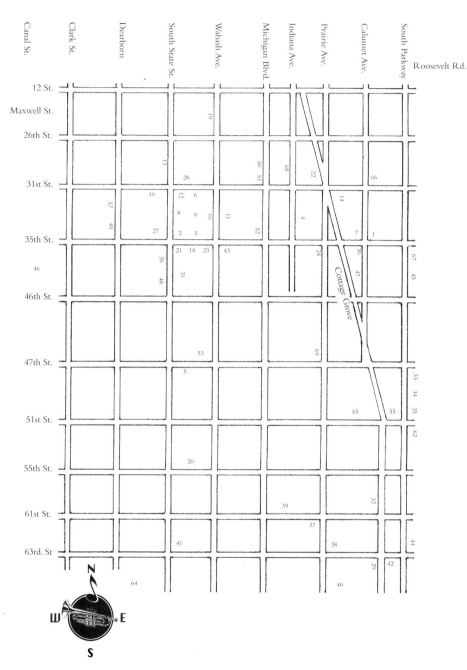

1. Al Tierney's Auto Inn; 35th & Calumet
2. Apex Club; 330 E. 35th St.
3. Avenue Theatre; 330 E. 35th St.
4. Blatz Beer Cafe; 3451 Indiana
5. Apollo Theatre; 526 E. 47th St.
6. Charleston Cafe (Royal Gardens); 459 E. 31st St.
7. Chatean Lounge; 35th & Calumet
8. Canton Tea Gardens; 404 S. Wabash
9. Colored Proff. Theater Club; 10 E. 32nd St.
10. Columbia Hotel; 4 W. 31st St.
11. Clarence Williams Publishing Co.; 33rd & Wabash
12. Dave Peyton's Music Shop; 3109 S. State St.
13. Belmont Cafe; 3035 S. State St.
14. Douglas Theatre; 3125 S. Cottage Grove
15. Dreamland Ballroom; 1701 W. Van Buren
16. Dusty Bottom (Tenet Dance Hall); 33rd & Wabash Ave.
17. Durks Record Shop; Maxwell St.
18. Entertainers Cafe (Glass bottom floor); 209 E. 35th St.
19. Freddy's Train Tavern; 2008 S. Wabash
20. Granada Cafe; 309 E. 55th St. (upstair)
21. Grand Terrance Ballroom (The Sunset Ballroom); 313 E. 35th St.
22. Groveland Theater; 31st & Cottage Grove
23. La Farancia Cafe; 215 E. 35th St.
24. Lorraine Gardens; 3501 S. Prairie
25. Mushmouth Johnson's; 464 S. State St.
26. Mexican Frank's Cafe; 3501 S. State St.
27. Pickford Theater; 108 E. 35th St.
28. Pompie Cafe; 20 E. 31st St.
29. Pershing Hotel (El Grotto Room); 64th & Cottage Grove
30. Mah Jong Cafe; 35th & Calumet
31. Masonia Temple; 3856 S. State St.
32. Trainon Ballroom
33. Tivoli Theater
34. McKies Lounge
35. Onyx Lounge
36. Parkway Bar; Pulaski Rd. & Washington Blvd.
37. Joe-Joe's Spitfire Club
38. Crown Propeller Lounge; Drexal Ave. & 63rd St.
39. Hour of Fantasy Club
40. The Urbanite Lounge
41. Elmers (3 piano bar); 63rd & State St.
42. White City Amusement Park; Cottage Grove & 63rd St.
43. Apex Club
44. Regal Theater; Parkway
45. Ritz Club; 3947 S. Parkway
46. Radio Inn; 39th & Vincennes
47. Ritz Carlton Restaurant; 3845 Cottage Grove Ave.
48. The Red Mill Cafe; 43rd & State St.
49. Rooming House (Ammons; Pine Top Smith; Lux Lewis; Others)
50. Savoy Hotel; 3000 S. Michigan Ave.
51. Savoy Cafe; 3010 S. Michigan Ave.
52. Schillers (old) Cafe; 35th & Michigan Ave.
53. Vendome Music Store (Erskine Tates); 47th & E. 31st
54. Savoy Ballroom
55. Warwick Hall
56. Massy Hall
57. Jimmy Yancey's House
58. Jazzland Park
59. New Orleans Babe's
60. 606 Club; S. State St.
61. The Hull House
62. Wendell Phillips High School
63. Crane Tech High School
64. Club DeLisa
65. Metrople Theatre
66. Shiller's Cafe
67. The Original; 3955 S. Parkway
68. Tuxedo Cafe; 3032 S. Indiana
69. 20th Century Theatre; 47th & Prairie

Above: During the Great Depression of the late 1920s and 1930s, many men were driven to sell apples on a corner. In this photograph, Chicago's mob boss, Al Capone, side steps a vet selling apples. (Demlinger Collection.)

At right: A tree poster advertises the Urbanite Restaurant and Lounge at 75th and Michigan Avenue. Dorothy Donegan was a well-known Chicago singer and pianist. (Demlinger Photograph.)

Within a few decades, Thomas A. Dorsey evolved from a blues composer and pianist for Ma Rainey to an internationally known choir leader and composer. Below, he is shown preparing his group for a national television show in the early 1960s. The photo at left shows the exterior of the church to which Dorsey belonged. (Steiner Collection.)

BURIED WITH CHRIST
IN BAPTISM

This photograph of State and 44th Street in the 1930s shows a huge poster announcing the appearance of Louis Armstrong and his orchestra at the Regal Theater. Note also Clarence Williams' Music Publishers across the street at 4404 South State. Williams not only wrote music but also recorded on Okeh records with his Clarence William's Blue Five, featuring Sidney Bechet and Louis Armstrong. Bechet's "Wild Cat Blues" is regarded by some as one of the greatest soprano sax solos ever recorded. Not far away, at 43rd Street, was the Red Mill, a club that offered music and dancing all night. (From Bill Russell.)

At left: This 1927 newspaper clipping belonged to Ralph Williams himself. Williams' orchestra played Chicago movie houses as well as clubs such as the Frolics. (Courtesy of Ralph Williams.)

Below: This c. 1966 photograph shows all that was left of the once-famous Frolics Show Lounge. The electric sign on top of the building once displayed its name. Ralph Williams' Orchestra played there in the 1920s, along with some other great jazzmen. When the heyday of booze and broads was over, the gangsters moved out. (Demlinger Photograph.)

Mama and Jimmy Yancey are pictured at home with Jimmy hitting some chords and playing his "Yancey Special." A boogie-woogie piano player, Yancey recorded on the Blue Note label and other jazz labels, including John Steiner's "new" Paramount label. His home on Dearborn Street was famous for hosting piano stylists who dropped in or visited from out of town. (Steiner Collection.)

A poster advertises the Four Tops and the Red Saunders' Orchestra, among others, at the Regal Theater. (Demlinger Photograph.)

The Regal Theater was billed as the best movie house in the United States. In the 1940s and 1950s, the Lionel Hampton and Dizzy Gillespie Orchestra, as well as other top bands, played the Regal. In the 1960s, the Regal was still featuring top stage talent such as The Four Tops, Karl Wright, and others. (Demlinger Photograph.)

In 1964, this humble graffiti appeared on a cement block wall in a South Side alley. "Bird Lives"—yes, in everyone's mind. (Demlinger Photograph.)

Chicagoan Meade "Lux" Lewis is pictured here at his piano. Lewis, along with Jimmy Yancey, brought a unique piano style to the public through recordings and performances at parties and clubs. (Steiner Collection.)

Meade "Lux" Lewis and Albert Ammons (foreground) play a duet on the Steinway. They had a regular duo act in Chicago clubs. Their boogie-woogie style would soon rocket them to stardom. (Steiner Collection.)

The Pershing Hotel on 64th and Cottage Grove Avenue featured some of the finest music on the entire South Side. It was not long after this photograph was taken in 1964 that the hotel was torn down. (Demlinger Photograph.)

The Metropolitan Theater showcased many of the top headliners of the day. Known locally as the Met, it was home to several bands including those led by King Oliver and Erskine Tate. (Demlinger Photograph.)

SAVOY BALLROOM
SOUTH PKWY. AT 47TH ST.
Thurs., Feb. 27th
CARNIVAL AND MASK BALL
SOUVENIRS FOR ALL
More Noise, Thrills, Joy
Dancing Every Thursday Eve.
and Sunday Matinee and Night

On Easter Sunday, the Savoy Ballroom offered continuous dancing from 4:30 p.m. on and featured Roy Eldridge and Lester Young—two bands on one billing. Much earlier, Louis Armstrong and his band played here, as well as Fletcher Henderson's band and Carroll Dickerson's orchestra. The ballroom was situated at 47th and South Parkway. In later years, this building became a supermarket. (Bill Russell Photograph.)

At left, an advertisement for the Savoy Ballroom highlights the "noise, thrills [and] joy" that could be found there.

At right, the Savoy News advertises its upcoming events.

SWING NUMBER | SPECIAL EDITION
SAVOY NEWS
VOL. 1   Chicago, Ill., Sunday, July 18 1937   No. 1
PUBLISHED IN THE INTEREST OF ENTERTAINMENT

Swing Parade
COMING TO SAVOY BALLROOM
SWING MASTERS COME TOGETHER IN ONE MASS SESSION

WHO'S TOPS IN SWING?

15 — BANDS — 15
IN A BATTLE OF SWING
EVERY THING SWINGS
To **SAVOY BALLROOM**
SUNDAY, JULY 18th

The White City bandstand often featured a "Battle of the Bands." This rare photograph from the Chuck Sullivan Collection shows the orchestra with jazz star Frank Teschemaker, one of the first members of the Austin High Gang, moustached in the center foreground. (Sullivan Collection.)

From the El platform at 63rd Street, one could see the sight of the famous White City Amusement Park. The park hosted a large bandstand and ballroom where many great dance orchestras of the 1920s and 1930s performed. White City was Chicago's Coney Island with high rides and roller coasters and all sorts of carnival buildings. Some older black residents recall that blacks in the city referred to this amusement park as for "Whites Only." The opposite postcard shows a romantic view of the 63rd Street entrance. (Demlinger Photograph.)

The South Side's Onyx Lounge featured top musicians. This photo was taken in 1963. (Demlinger Photograph.)

The Metropole Hotel, at Michigan and 23rd Street, had a lounge, dining area, and large dance floor where local bands played. In the 1920s, Al Capone would allegedly frequent the Metropole at a rate of $1,500 a day. It was rumored that the Metropole was run by the mob. (Demlinger Photograph.)

This building at 60th and Cottage Grove Avenue was originally the Midway Gardens Ballroom. Like the Dreamland, the Midway hosted some of the finest musicians including Muggsy Spanier, Benny Goodman, Jimmie Palmers, Mel Cole, and Eddie Wiggins. (Steiner Collection.)

The Owl Theater, pictured here in 1964, featured movies and musical acts. Glover Compton is reputed to have accompanied films on the piano here. (Demlinger Photograph.)

The Grand Terrace at 3955 South Parkway was a swinging place with the bands of Earl Hines, Carroll Dickerson, and Count Basie coming in for weekly shows. Fletcher Henderson's large orchestra opened the New Grand Terrace, at 35th and Calumet Avenue. Along with the Count Basie Band, the Earl Hines Orchestra entertained there for many years. (Bill Russell Photograph.)

The Warwick Hall at 543 East 47th Street held conventions, meetings, and club dances. Concerts on weekends featured the bands of Natty Dominique, Jimmie Noone, and others. Nat King Cole also played at the Warwick early in his career. It was still being used here in the early 1940s. (From Bill Russell.)

John Steiner took this wonderful photograph, at right, of bassist George "Pops" Foster, Mrs. Darnell Howard, and clarinetist Darnell Howard. Pops Foster played the bass in many bands fronted by Bunk Johnson of New Orleans fame.

In the background of this 1961 image is a medical center that used to be the famous Panama Café, and next door, upstairs from the barbershop, was the very famous café called the DeLuxe. Darnell and Foster both remembered Louis and Jabbo Smith blowin' up a storm at these clubs. It is interesting to note that Darnell Howard is facing the site of the Dreamland Ballroom.

Pictured is a "pre-Valentine dance" poster for El Sid's Ballroom, formerly the Trainon Ballroom, on Cottage Grove Avenue. The photo was taken in 1966. (Demlinger Photograph.)

53

Smitty's Corner was typical of taverns where music could be heard for the price of a beer. A South Side double store at 35th and Indiana, Smitty's Corner hosted Muddy Waters with a blues band for years. (Steiner Collection.)

Chicago's South Side paper, the Chicago Defender, featured a "Show Business" section that advertised blues and jazz recordings. This page, at right, included a c. 1920 ad from the Michigan Theater (above), which was located at 55th and Michigan. (Demlinger Photograph.)

Here is a slightly worn photograph of a group at the Apex Club around 1951. Ralph Hutchinson, not pictured, was on trombone, Tut Soper is seen on piano, Muggsy Dawson on cornet, and Bud Jacobson on clarinet. The drummer is unidentified. (Photo by Merit Jacobson.)

The Club DeLisa was one of several popular lounges on the South Side. Headlining on this day in 1964 were B.B. King, Johnny Williams, and Joann Garrett. The emcee was Carl Wright. (Demlinger Photograph.)

The Tivoli Theater featured live performers, vaudeville acts, and name orchestras. This photo is c. 1928. (Demlinger Collection.)

The famous McKie's Show Lounge, next to the Tivoli Theater, had weekly jazz sessions. In this photograph, tenor man Illinois Jacquet was the headliner. (Steiner Collection.)

The Grand Theater stood next to the Tivoli Theater on the South Side. (Steiner Collection.)

Here is the famous Roberts Show Club, pictured in 1966. It hosted some of the best Chicago blues and jazz. (Demlinger Photograph.)

The Grand Terrace, formerly the Sunset, was home to great jazz bands like those led by Fletcher Henderson, Count Basie, and Earl Hines. (Steiner Collection.)

The Southerland Hotel's lounge featured top jazz players during its time. On the bill when this photograph was taken in 1969 was Bill Henderson, with Nancy Wilson soon to arrive. (Steiner Photograph.)

The Michigan Hotel had a show lounge on its corner called the Barclay. It featured small combos and solo pianists. (Demlinger Photograph.)

In the 1930s and 1940s, 606 Club at 606 South Wabash Avenue featured small swing and jazz bands like Joe Marek's. (Steiner Photograph.)

OPPOSITE: *During the 1940s and 1950s, Jo-Joe's Spitfire Lounge, a short-lived club on the city's South Side, featured everything from be-bop to swing to Latin music. (Demlinger Photograph.)*

STAGE-MUS

PAGE EIGHT   ★   RELIABLE FOR 24

Hal Bakay and Boyd Atkins at Club Ritz Sunday Night

This Sunday night, Feb. 23, the Club Ritz will have 'its formal opening with Hal Bakay as master of ceremonies on a bill of elaborate entertainment featured by Boyd Atkins' famous Vagabonds orchestra.

This announcement should be of interest to those who have frequented the beautiful Ritz ballroom, and the fact that Bakay will do the honors lends a zest to the affair which will draw many of his admirers.

In addition to Bakay and Atkins' band, dazzling Ruby Mason will act as hostess. Anybody who has ever seen this vivacious and clever girl work knows that Texas Guinan has little on her. Besides Ruby there

AT THE REGAL
By CORIENNE ROBINSON

"THE THIRTEENTH CHAIR" for mystery and "The Laughing Lady" for drama mean another week of perfect entertainment at the Regal, with two shows, starting Saturday, Feb. 22, and Wednesday, Feb. 26, respectively.

STRANGE MYSTERIES in a ghostly room, voices from the great beyond, the exposing of mediumistic tricks and the dramatic solution of a baffling mystery—it's all in "The Thirteenth Chair."

"MADAME X" set a new mark in screen technique and "The Thirteenth Chair," Ted Browning's all-talking sensation of the Veiller mystery drama, sets a new mark for mystery stories on the screen.

CONRAD NAGEL and Leila Hyams play the romantic leads in the new play, working out a romance amid the mystery, and Bela Lugosi, who played

On the Stroll By Ace

Did you know that two men of our group are responsible for the big song hits, "Am I Blue" and "Through"? I didn't, and maybe they aren't, but so says a letter to this department. Somebody who knows, check me up on this, will you?

'Dark Wings' to Be Given on March 3

"Dark Wings," a comedy version of the aviator's part in love and war, will be produced at the Eighth St. theater, under the auspices of the Universal Aviation association Monday evening, March 3.

Carnival and Mask Ball at the Savoy

Pictured above, the Chicago Defender's page eight lists many of the city's hottest gigs. (Steiner Collection.)

Pictured below is a rare copy of the Bronzeville Gazette, telling about the coming "Swing Out" between Benny Goodman and Roy Eldridge. "Appearing at the Eighth Street Armory, 'specially air cooled, for your dancing pleasure. The bands will go neck to neck, and feature Teddy Wilson, Lionel Hampton, and Gene Krupa, while Eldridge is banking." (Steiner Collection.)

SWING FANS WELCOME TO BRONZEVILLE

Swing Convention Special

THE BRONZEVILLE GAZETTE

National Edition

VOLUME 2   JUNE 22, 1937   Number 6

PUBLISHED BY THE BRONZEVILLE BOOSTER'S CLUB, 543 E. 47th STREET, CHICAGO, ILL.   PHONE DREXEL 6339

BENNY GOODMAN & ROY ELDRIDGE "SWING OUT" IN CHICAGO JUNE 22

—The Swing Master

"Swing Convention" Biggest Event In Dance History

Teddy Wilson, Lionel Hampton, Gene Krupa and Peg La Centra Starred With Swingmaster

ELDRIDGE IS BANKING ON CLEO BROWN AND ZUTTY

With the 8th Regiment Armory 'specially decorated and air-cooled . . . with Benny Goodman and his clarinet all ready to go . . . Teddy Wilson's fingers . . .

—Pride of Bronzeville

The 1965 offices of the Chicago Defender *newspaper are pictured above. An earlier building suffered a fire, which destroyed everything, including their photography collection. (Demlinger Photograph.)*

The Chicago Defender's *"Show Business" section the week of February 13, 1930, highlights a rousing event featuring Louis Armstrong and 50 famous stars from the movie and theater world appearing at the Savoy Ballroom. The Regal Theater allowed its band leader, Dave Peyton, and his orchestra to appear alternately with Bernie Young's band. The article notes that this would be a super event, as Louis Armstrong said this would be his only showing in Chicago for a very long time. (Steiner Collection.)*

Louis Armstrong Will Be Feature at Theatrical Ball

The popular Savoy ballroom announces what promises to be the biggest event ever held within the portals of the ballroom Thursday night, Feb. 13, with the outstanding attraction being none other than the boy who made Broadway eat out of the palm of his hand this past year and whom Broadway now has its hand stretched out awaiting his return, Louis Armstrong, hailed far and wide as the greatest master of the trumpet that ever lived.

Honoring this great special theatrical ball there will be more than 50 famous stars of the theatrical world who will take part in this huge event destined to be the greatest yet held in the ballroom where many great balls have already taken place.

Two of Chicago's greatest orchestras will furnish the music for the dancing, which starts at 9 and will continue until the wee small hours of the morning. The Regal theater has finally consented to the appearance of its crack orchestra, which, in theatrical circles, is the rage, and Dave Peyton and his boys will hold forth that night in a veritable frenzy of jazz, alternating with Bernie Young and his orchestra, which certainly needs no introduction to readers of this column.

Stage stars from all walks of life, from Loop theaters, from Broadway, from Hollywood and from our own Chicago are wiring in for reservations, and many of your old favorites along with many new faces will join in the festivities that night, making it a sweetheart of a time for every sweetie and his sweetheart.

The Savoy will be gaudily decorated for the occasion and the great Louis Armstrong, favorite of favorites in Chicago, is priming himself for 'tis final Chicago engagement, for 'tis said that it will be his first and only engagement in Chicago for many and many a year. It is hoped that all Chicago will turn out in full force to honor this youth who goes out into the great white way and conquers the hearts of millions.

This June 1949 concert at the Terrace Garden consisted of an all-time Dixieland trumpet section. Pictured here, from left to right, are Doc Evans, Lee Collins, Jimmy McPartland, and Bunk Johnson. (From Doc Evans.)

This is a rare photograph of Bunk Johnson, the famous New Orleans trumpeter. He stayed at John Steiner's home for weeks while playing in Chicago. (Steiner Collection.)

The Dallas Bartley Band played all over Chicago's South Side as well as points outside the Windy City. (Steiner Collection.)

Jimmy Noone plays his clarinet to the amusement of four cross-dressers at the Cabin Inn. (Steiner Collection/Courtesy of Frank Driggs.)

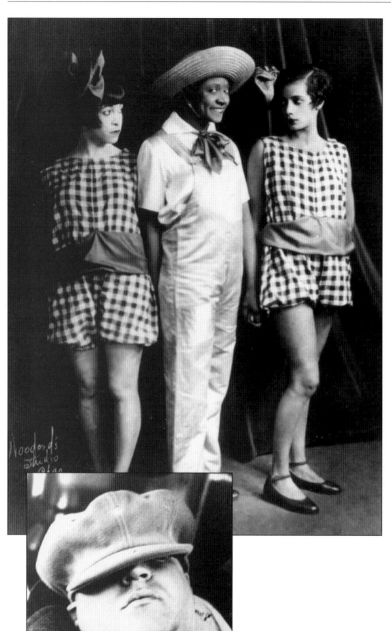

Three famous wives line up for the Woodwards Studio in Chicago. They are, from left to right, Katherine Perry (Mrs. Earl Hines), Eloise Bennett (Mrs. C. Scott), and Irene Eadie (Mrs. Teddy Wilson). In 1927, they worked private parties at the Sunset and Café de Paris. (Steiner Collection.)

Here is a slumbering Tommy Ladiner. A great trumpet player, Tommy played on several Sidney Bechet and Jelly Roll Morton records. (Steiner Collection.)

John Steiner and Lil Hardin Armstrong on the steps of the house where she and Louis lived in Chicago. Lil is holding sheet music. (Demlinger Photograph.)

This dramatic photograph, taken from high above the El tracks on Chicago's South Side, looks down on a night club situated next door to a hotel. This was a standard arrangement, as there were many waitresses in the night club, and a direct exit to the hotel next door made for a potentially hot night. (Steiner Collection.)

Before they played the theater circuit, famous blues and spiritual singers of the day such as Bessie Smith, Lizzie Miles, Ma Rainey, and Sara Martin performed in tents like these on Chicago's South Side. People would go to the tents to get a closer look and to feel the music and the singing. (Steiner Photograph.)

George Dixon's All-Star Combo could be heard in many small clubs dotting the South Side and Near North Side during the 1940s and early 1950s. (Steiner Collection.)

Drummer Red Saunders was a feature at the Club DeLisa for many years. He and his band backed many top headliners. (Demlinger Collection.)

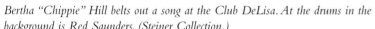

Bertha "Chippie" Hill belts out a song at the Club DeLisa. At the drums in the background is Red Saunders. (Steiner Collection.)

This is one of the only known photographs of the Crown Propeller Lounge, which was located at 68 East 63rd Street at Drexel Avenue. It was home to be-bop giants from 1940 to 1960. (Demlinger Photograph.)

CHAPTER FOUR
Downtown
1920s–1960s

CHICAGO'S DOWNTOWN was a focal point of the jazz craze as most of the downtown hotels, restaurants, lounges, and nightspots all had some form of music. In addition, all the theaters downtown had orchestras and bands that either played in the pits or were themselves featured. They would also play background for the stage acts and performers.

The music scene in downtown Chicago played to a cosmopolitan crowd. At the Bismarck Hotel, for example, large dinners costing $2 or more were served for the after theater crowd. A small band would play waltz music or two-step. The Drake Hotel featured Clyde McCoy and his orchestra with the newest ideas in sounds. The Moulin Rouge Café at 416 South Wabash had eight course dinners for $1.50 and dance music by James Wade's Syncopators.

The various hotels throughout the downtown area offered a fine assortment of jazz options. The College Inn at the Hotel Sherman, one of the most preeminent hotels and a leading night-life venue in Chicago, had an on-going love affair with all kinds of music. You could hear the great sounds of many orchestras including those of Duke Ellington, Gene Krupa, and Benny Goodman. In the basement of the Hotel Sherman was the famous Panther Room. Here, some of the greatest musicians of all time played and recorded. From Count Basie to Fats Waller to Louis Armstrong to Frank Sinatra, the Panther Room hosted some of the hottest talent.

The Palmer House featured soft listening jazz music for dining customers. In the hotel's Victoria Room, Freddie Meiken could be found performing. Meiken wrote "The Wabash Blues," which was originally titled "The Trombone Blues." He was paid $50 for the music, but later the music publisher settled for a much larger amount. Others who appeared at the Victoria Room included violinist Lou Alberti, trombonist Marc Schartz, and Jess Barnes. During late night dinners, pianist Mel Rosenberg and violinist James Garfield Haenschel delighted all. They were not hot jazz players, but they could liven up the evening when asked to.

Much has been written about another famed Chicago night spot, the Three Deuces (222 North State Street) and its owner, Sam Beers. Sam learned all he could by waiting on customers from behind his own bar. The bar was on the left as you entered, and he placed a small piano in back of the bar, rather than a large one in the center among the tables where he could seat only a few customers. This proved more intimate for a lot of the patrons who could then be hustled for drinks.

The upstairs bar was about 75-feet long with tables and booths opposite the bar and a small booth to the left of the entrance where entertainers sat during intermission or greeted customers as they entered. In the earliest years, Sam paid $5 to a pianist for a Saturday "audition," which would last all night. If he was great and drew patrons, the musician was offered the grand total of $5 nightly, until things got better. Legend has it that when the agent for the local union checked on what was going on at the Three Deuces, he would be told the performer had been given the night off to settle a bar bill.

Joints like this would jockey for every inch of space. The Three Deuces had a very low ceiling in the basement, since it was originally a storage place. In order for a band to play, the stage was raised about 10 inches above the floor, which brought the ceiling so close that they cut a well in the floor to allow an upright bass fiddle to fit. The stage itself had just enough room for a drum, a bass (in its well), a piano, guitar, and three chairs tightly packed together. When Roy Eldridge brought in his band, there was no room for him so he had to stand down on the floor, off stage.

Chicago's downtown had its share of fine lounges and bars such as the Brass Rail, the Capitol Show lounge, and the great Blue Note, with its ample stage for large orchestras to perform. On Wacker Drive, there were

DOWNTOWN
AS OF 1930

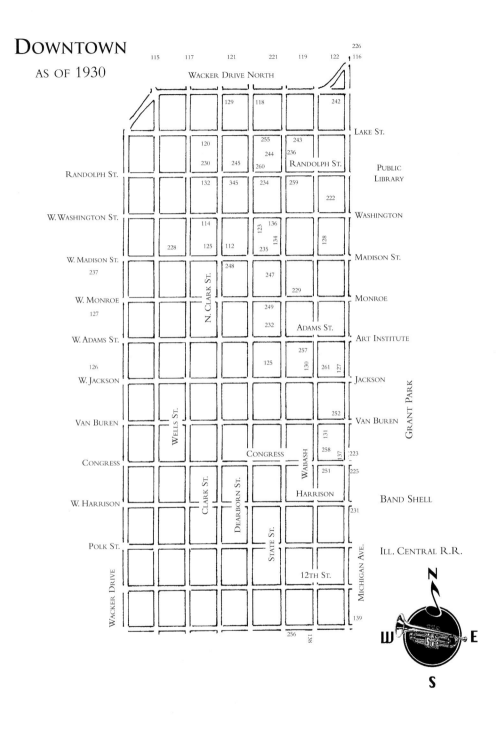

WACKER DRIVE NORTH

LAKE ST.

RANDOLPH ST.

RANDOLPH ST.

PUBLIC LIBRARY

W. WASHINGTON ST.

WASHINGTON

W. MADISON ST.

MADISON ST.

W. MONROE

MONROE

W. ADAMS ST.

ADAMS ST.

ART INSTITUTE

W. JACKSON

JACKSON

VAN BUREN

VAN BUREN

GRANT PARK

CONGRESS

CONGRESS

HARRISON

BAND SHELL

W. HARRISON

POLK ST.

12TH ST.

ILL. CENTRAL R.R.

N. CLARK ST. — WELLS ST. — CLARK ST. — DEARBORN ST. — STATE ST. — WABASH — MICHIGAN AVE. — WACKER DRIVE

CLUBS

112. The Blue Note
113. Lipps Lower Level
114. Brass Rail
115. The Rag Doll
116. The Drake Hotel; Michigan & Lake Shore Dr.
117. *Chez* Parie
118. The Three Deuces
119. The Esquire Club
120. The Glass Hat
121. Silver Frolics
122. The London House; Wacker Dr. & Michigan Ave.
123. The Palace Theater
124. United Artists (Apollo) Theater
125. Rialto Theater
126. The Opera House
127. The Civic Theater
128. The Black Hawk; 139 N. Wabash
129. Dublins Records; Wacker Dr.
130. Rose Records; Wabash Ave.
131. Seymours Record Mart; Wabash Ave.
132. The College Inn (Sherman Hotel)
133. The Palmer House
134. The Roosevelt Theater
135. The Chateau LaMar Cafe
137. The Friars Inn (New Orleans Rhythm Kings)
138. The Chicago Stock Yard Inn
139. The Coliseum; S. Michigan Ave.

HOTELS: DINE AND DANCE

221. Ambassador East (Pump Room); State & Goethe
222. Black Hawk; 139 N. Wabash
223. Blackstone Hotel; Michigan Ave. at 7th St.
225. Congress Hall (The Glass Hat); Congress & Michigan Ave.
226. The Drake Hotel (Camellia House); Michigan & Lake Shore Dr.
227. Edgewater Beach Hotel (Marine Room); 5349 N. Sheridan Rd.
228. LaSalle Hotel (Lotus Room); Madison & LaSalle
229. Palmer House (Empire Room); 15 E. Monroe
230. Sherman Hotel (College Inn); Clark & Randolph St.
231. Stevens Hotel (Blvd. Room); 720 S. Michigan Ave.
232. Bismarck Hotel
235. North American Restaurant; State & Monroe St.
236. Capital; 167 N. State
237. Streamliner; W. Madison & Clinton
238. *Chez* Parie
239. Esquire
240. The Glass Hat
242. The London House
255. The Three Deuces

THEATERS (WITH ORCHESTRAS)

243. The Chicago
244. State & Lake
245. Oriental
246. Palace
247. McVickers
248. United Artists (Apollo)
249. Roosevelt
251. Blackstone
252. Orchestra Hall

This photograph shows Chicago's downtown on State Street in 1928. Al Jolson appeared in the first "talking picture show," The Jazz Singer, announced on the Castle Theater marquee at far left. One can almost hear the clank of the streetcar on its way to the Union Stock Yards. Further on is the Roosevelt Theater where Harold Lloyd appeared in a silent comedy, and the State and Lake Theater, offering vaudeville billing. Across the street from the State and Lake Theater is the Chicago Theater—the only theater from this era remaining downtown. In the right foreground is the Carson Pirie Scott department store. (Demlinger Collection.)

Pictured above is Joe Marsala and his Chicagoans. (Steiner Collection.)

At left: According to notes John Steiner took while visiting Chicago clubs, the Showboat Lounge was the busiest and last of a group of hot spots south of the Loop on State Street. The area, once primarily working class, declined to a mini-skid row and eventually the lounge vanished altogether. The Showboat was known for a trio that would play for eight hours from a stage behind the bar. Bud Jacobson's talents were preeminent because he could serve as the swing member of groups. He played the instruments in succession: reeds, piano, and then drums during other members' off-times. (Steiner Collection.)

two important jazz spots, one of which was an upstairs lounge called the Gaffers Club. Here, Bud Freeman and Joe Thomas held court for a long time. The other lounge was the London House on the city's windiest corner on Michigan Avenue and Wacker Drive.

Along State Street there was a theater on every block and Chicago's loop held its own with New York's Broadway. These theaters featured some of the hottest jazz and many of the best musicians.

The Loop was also home to many of the leading music publishers who recorded much of the early jazz music. The most important was the recording studio at 227 West Washington, where Okeh Records did their recording. Also notable was the Melrose recording studios and publishers at 177 North State Street. The Lyon and Healy Company, famous for their pianos, also recorded in their building for the Victor Record Company.

Over time, Chicago's downtown hosted music from every jazz form, from Dixieland and New Orleans-style to big band, swing, and be-bop.

This 1912 photograph shows Chicago's Palmer House on the left near State and Monroe Streets. On the right side was the DeJonghe Hotel, which catered to the dance music of the day with a small orchestra in the dining room. On the corner of State Street was the North American Restaurant, featuring violin music by James Garfield Haenschel and piano from Mel Rosenberg. (Demlinger Collection.)

This 1920s view shows Orchestra Hall on Michigan Avenue, which featured concerts by symphonic orchestras as well as bands, which played between movies. In later years, when air conditioning was brought in, there were real jazz concerts on special days. (Demlinger Collection.)

Downtown's Wabash Avenue had a string of fine food establishments that featured music for dancing. At the Blackhawk, located on the southeast corner of Randolph and Wabash, fine music sounds were provided by Red Norvo, Bob Crosby and his large orchestra, Coon Sanders, and—as the sign says—Art Jarrett and his orchestra. (Demlinger Photograph.)

This view north on State Street in 1927 shows Harold Lloyd on the bill at the Roosevelt Theater. Looming ever larger were the State and Lake and the Chicago Theaters. Today, only the Chicago Theater remains. (Demlinger Collection.)

Appearing on the bill at the Chicago Theater c. 1933 was Cab Calloway and his Cotton Club Orchestra, along with a Jack Oakie film Shoot the Works. *This was a weekly episode at the large movie houses—a headliner orchestra or act plus a movie or play. This early photograph shows the 1933 World's Fair Century of Progress banner hanging over the marquee along with several American flags. (Steiner Collection.)*

This April 13, 1926 photograph shows the marquee advertising Al Jolson, who was appearing in the stage hit Big Boy *at the Apollo Theater, later named the United Artist Theater. Only two years later, Al Jolson made history when he appeared in the first talking motion picture,* The Jazz Singer. *(Demlinger Collection.)*

Downtown's McVickers Theater, located at 23 West Madison Street, was playing the hit movie Ukulele Ike *when this photograph was taken. Ralph Williams' Orchestra played the intermission with his large ensembles. (Courtesy of Ralph Williams.)*

The famous Three Deuces at 222 North State Street near Lake Street. (Demlinger Collection.)

The Friars Inn, below, was home to some great jazz bands including George Brunies and the Café Society Orchestra. (Steiner Collection.)

The Friars Inn on Congress Street was home to many historic jazz bands, including the New Orleans Rhythm Kings. In 1922, the band featured Ben Pollack, drums; George Brunies, trombone; Paul Mares, trumpet; Leon Rappolo, clarinet; Elmer Schoebel, piano; Jack Pettis, saxophone; Lew Black, guitar; and Steve Brown on bass. This 1930s snapshot by Bill Russell shows the exterior of the Friars Inn from across the street. (Demlinger Collection.)

One-armed trumpeter Wingy Manone plays his own style of Dixieland music. In addition to his singing, Manone entertained the crowd with his stage presence. Pianist Don Ewell is on the left. (Steiner Collection.)

The Brass Rail had fine musical lineups year round. It hosted traditional New Orleans jazz and, in the 1950s, Count Basie and his Orchestra. The group consisted of Basie on piano, Gus Johnson on drums, Jimmy Lewis on bass, Bob Graf on tenor, Clark Terry on trumpet, and Buddy DeFranco on clarinet—talk about a swinging bunch! (Steiner Collection.)

Dave Brubeck plays in concert with drummer Joe Morello. (Demlinger Photograph.)

The great Bob Crosby Orchestra of the 1940s had this lineup of stars: Muggsy Spanier on cornet and Eddie Miller on saxophone with Bob standing to the far right. (Steiner Collection.)

The entire Abe Lyman Orchestra poses for a formal portrait for the Brunswick record company's promotion department. The Orchestra often played at the large Chicago hotel ballrooms. (Steiner Collection.)

One of the many sweet bands that played the hotel and dance circuits around Chicago was the Sig Meyer band. This bunch of musicians was called Sig Meyer and his Druids. (Steiner Collection.)

OPPOSITE: *Bunk Johnson had just arrived in Chicago on a late night in September of 1946 (according to legend, with his ticket envelope still in his pocket) to play a scheduled concert in his honor at Orchestra Hall. Bunk, arriving after the concert had started, had no rehearsal time or even a warm-up. Some who were there have said that half the audience left feeling they had been conned; while the other half left inspired with the feeling that they had been a part of jazz history.*

The bass player, John Lindsay, was known in earlier days as an outstanding trombonist playing with the bands of Oliver, Morton, and Armstrong. He became a premier bassman in his later years. Clifford "Snags" Jones, the drummer, was named for his "toothiness" and had been active in Chicago since the early 1920s. He was an eccentric rhythmist like Jasper Taylor and Baby Dodds. Don Ewell was the pianist.

The others on stage (not shown) were Darnell Howard on clarinet, Lee Collins on trumpet, Preston Jackson on trombone, and Lonnie Johnson on guitar.

Bunk remained in town for months, often appearing unannounced to jam in the clubs on Clark Street. He lived with Dave Bell, the owner of Session Record Mart, who was an ardent admirer of Bunk. Mama Yancey was their housekeeper. Bunk had been known to entertain guests in his longjohns. (Steiner Collection.)

It was March 18, 1949, when this photograph was taken of Doc Evans on cornet, Joyce McDonald, Johnny McDonald, Doc Cenardo, and Al Jenkins on trombone. (From Doc Cenardo.)

This photograph shows the Metronome All-Stars, which was made up of the best jazz players of 1948–49. Among them are Buddy DeFranco, taking a solo on clarinet; next to him are Charlie Parker and Charlie Ventura on the sax; J.J. Johnson on trombone along with Kai Winding; Miles Davis, Dizzy Gillespie, and Fats Navarro made up the trumpet section; Shelly Mann on drums; Eddie Safranski on bass; Billy Bauer on guitar; and Lennie Tristano on piano. (Steiner Collection.)

In 1932, the Chateau LaMar in 1932 had a knock-out lineup that played for dancing. The band included Dick Donahue and Johnny Mendel on trumpet; Floyd O'Brien and Eddie Kusborsky on trombone; Tut Soper on piano; and Joe Mack. (Steiner Collection.)

The Frankie Trumbauer Orchestra is pictured here in 1932. (Duncan Schiedt Collection.)

Dancing to the music of Isham Jones at the Hotel Sherman's College Inn was a treat for folks in the 1930s. The Panther Room was also at the hotel and here luminaries such as Duke Ellington and Gene Krupa played. (Steiner Collection.)

Duke Ellington's orchestra frequently visited the Hotel Sherman's Panther Room. Here, one of his orchestra's most unique musicians, Ray Nance, is shown playing the violin. (Steiner Collection.)

Jimmie McPartland is seen here at the mike belting out a song. (From Mr. and Mrs. Frank J. Gillis.)

CHAPTER FIVE

Near North Side

1920s–1960s

THE CHICAGO RIVER is the dividing line between the Near North Side and Chicago's downtown. There was a lot going on in this area with major hotels, great places to dine, and hundreds of bars lining the streets.

Rush Street was host to many fine food restaurants and clubs that had dancing and entertainment. In the 1920s, a place called Kelly's Stables offered drinks and hot jazz that featured Johnny Dodds and his New Orleans style of music. The Stables was a real stable that had sawdust on the floor, wooden tables, and a black-painted interior. They served hard booze and handmade beer. It was particularly attractive to the budding movie colony in Chicago. Kelly even quoted D.W. Griffith, the famous movie director, as saying, "I got the jazzy inspiration to produce *That Royal Girl*, while visiting Kelly's Stables. I consider this place the real Chicago nightlife atmosphere."

Another stand-out club on the Near North Side was the Club Alabam. It would draw in huge crowds because of the fine food and chorus line, as well as a featured act. The Club Alabam's review had such stars as Evelyn Nesbitt and her fine stage act or Earl Tucker and the Harlem Follies. Plus, they all had fine dance bands to go along with their shows. The orchestra that played on weekends was named the Alabamians for obvious reasons, but its personnel changed nightly. Rupnecks up on Rush Street catered to those who required the best of foods. It had a small dance floor and dance band.

North Clark Street featured bar after bar all the way north to Fullerton. One of the early dancehalls on Clark Street was the Frank O'Donnell's Bar. Downstairs it was a bar, but upstairs there was an entire floor for the band and dancers. The sign was still there in late 1950s. Up above the Standard Theater was another dancehall with a side door entrance. Along Clark Street was the famous Victory Club, made famous because New Orleans musician Lee Collins often played there. Here, hip college students would drop in from the Chicago area campuses to listen to all of the hot jazz music.

Over at the Sky Club, they were hot to trot to Johnny Lane and his sidekick George Brunies who at this time was staying at hotel on the far West Side of town. When World War II was in full swing, the servicemen would come into Chicago and head straight for the Clark Street bars and strip joints. At this time, they all had live bands backing the girls. Usually hidden behind flimsy curtains would be some outstanding jazz musicians who would take almost any job.

Clark Street's Hi-Note Lounge featured Anita O'Day for weeks and weeks as everyone in the city loved her. On Erie Street there was the Drum Lounge and the Erie Club. The Airliner Club was a hot jazz place for months on end and brought in some top talents and crowds to match. On Division and Wells Streets, the House of Fantasy played with all sorts of rhythms from Latin jazz to Congo music.

Jazz Ltd. was home to some of the best jazz found anywhere. Ruth and Bill Reinhardt owned this basement club and made it one of the best in the land. On certain nights, it would feature Big Sid Catlett on drums, Floyd O'Brien on trombone, and Don Ewell or Wally Rose on piano with Bill Reinhardt himself sitting in the clarinet chair. But what made it all so wonderful was the fact that Sidney Bechet, the soprano sax master, was there for a long stay. But then one day, with only two weeks left on his contract, Bechet called Bill on the telephone from New York and told him he was leaving for Paris, France, and would never return. The Reinhardt's filled his seat with Muggsy Spanier, who also stayed on for a long time.

I had a chance to talk to Bechet while he was there, and during a break, he told me that he hated to play to people just sitting there and listening. He liked it when people would get up and dance to the happy music he was making, even if it was the blues. Bechet had come back to the United

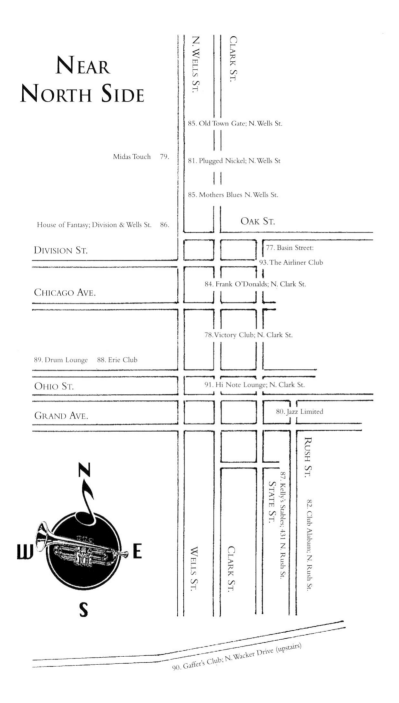

NEAR
NORTH SIDE

N. WELLS ST.

CLARK ST.

85. Old Town Gate; N. Wells St.

Midas Touch 79.

81. Plugged Nickel; N. Wells St

85. Mothers Blues N. Wells St.

OAK ST.

House of Fantasy; Division & Wells St. 86.

DIVISION ST.

77. Basin Street:

93. The Airliner Club

CHICAGO AVE.

84. Frank O'Donalds; N. Clark St.

78. Victory Club; N. Clark St.

89. Drum Lounge   88. Erie Club

OHIO ST.

91. Hi Note Lounge; N. Clark St.

GRAND AVE.

80. Jazz Limited

RUSH ST.

N

W   E

S

WELLS ST.

CLARK ST.

87. Kelly's Stables; 431 N. Rush St.

STATE ST.

82. Club Alabam; N. Rush St.

90. Gaffer's Club; N. Wacker Drive (upstairs)

States in 1947. He had been overseas since 1918. He started playing professionally in 1910 when he joined the Olympic Band in New Orleans. Years later, it was a sad day when Jazz Ltd. closed its door for the last time.

The places along Wells Street had storefronts for everything. The Old Town Gate provided for Franz Jackson and his New Orleans style band. This three-story building lit up the night sky for everyone to see. Franz Jackson could play his clarinet like the best New Orleans had to offer, and he surrounded himself with great talented artists. The Plugged Nickel, which was a little false front building, catered to jazz lovers of every sort and brought in the best talent in the world. They even had jam sessions in the afternoons, and talents from top comics like Red Fox to the singers Carmen McRae, Nina Simone, and Gloria Lynn.

The best of be-bop played there too—Sonny Stitt, Dizzy Gillespie—you name it. Just down the street was a place called Mother Blues. Singing and playing there would be the talents of B.B. King, Bob Gibson, or Big Bill Broonzey. Across the street from the Old Town Gate was a place called the Midas Touch that had signs all over the building proclaiming jazz and jam sessions on Sundays. Appearing there one week in 1967 was Judy Roberts. This club faced a real obstacle going up against a place like the Plugged Nickel, whose owners knew jazz talent when they heard it.

On Division Street near Oak Street was a jazz place called Basin Street. Here Muggsy Spanier and George Brunies led a great Dixieland band in a place that resembled a New Orleans club. Later, it started a Latin music trend to bring in more customers. A few doors down stood the Monte Carlo Club, which also advertised jam sessions three nights a week. Just north of the Victory Club was the building that housed the Liberty Inn. The Gate of Horn was Chicago's center of folk music, which featured acts such as Peter, Paul and Mary early in their careers.

The Near North Side was bustling with activity and entertainment. Today, the area remains a center of Chicago's exciting nightlife.

Basin Street, far right, a swinging jazz and blues lounge, featured many types of music during its history. Here, as seen in 1967, it played mambo and cha cha music, but a few years earlier, it played great Dixieland jazz. This photo was taken on State Street near Oak Street. The Monte Carlo, far left, held a jam session on the weekends with local Chicago musicians. (Demlinger Photograph.)

A great Dixie jam session headed by George Brunies and Muggsy Spanier plays at a packed house at Basin Street. (Steiner Collection.)

This early winter 1961 shot of Early Murphy on the bass, Brian Shanley on the clarinet, and Muggsy Spanier on trumpet, was taken at the Basin Street Club on State Street. Toward the end of the great revival, veterans were in short supply and new talent like clarinetist Brian Shanley found opportunities to work with the great leaders. Like several other players of his period, Shanley learned jazz at the University of Wisconsin. (Steiner Collection.)

At right, George Brunies, Muggsy Spanier, and Brian Shanley take center stage at Basin Street. (Steiner Collection.)

The House of Fantasy was a show club and lounge at Division and Wells Streets that featured small bands. Sometimes boppers Red Rodney, Coltrane, and Mulligan played there. By the late 1950s, it was already a shadow of what it had been. (Demlinger Photograph.)

Mother Blues was on North Wells Street. On the bill at the time of this photo was Bob Gibson with Spanky and Our Gang. B.B. King, Big Bill Broonzy, and other blues singers performed at Mother Blues as well. (Demlinger Photograph.)

The Standard Theater offered triple features in the early 1950s in order to stay afloat. Years earlier, you could use the side entrance, walk up the stairs, and enter a fairly large dancehall, complete with a good dance band that would play "Cake Walk" or a waltz. (Demlinger Photograph.)

Natty Dominique played the trumpet for Johnny Dodds' group at Kelly's Stables and other significant jobs. The below photograph shows him with his nephew Don Albert. Don recorded respected jazz groups from the 1920s into the 1950s (even though he is not a Chicagoan). This photograph was taken in Steiner-Davis Records' studio A. (Steiner Photograph.)

At right: The autograph on this photo reads, "To Annabelle & Junice Cobb—Two terrific performers— it's been grand working on the same bill with you. Bette Andre." (Steiner Collection.)

Below: Mike McKendrick (left) and Marty Gross play a guitar duet for the camera. (Steiner Photograph.)

Above: This swinging group of musicians includes, from left to right, Earl Murphy on bass, Volly DeFaut on clarinet, Doc Evans on cornet, and Al Jenkins on trombone. (Duncan Schiedt Collection.)

This great group of musicians includes, from left to right, an unidentified bass player, Baby Dodds at the drums, pianist Don Ewell (standing), Jimmie Noone holding his clarinet, and Roy Eldridge with his trumpet. (Steiner Collection.)

During the 1920s, Club Alabam hosted talented stage shows that featured acts such as Evelyn Nesbitt, Ted Lewis, and other stage personalities. (Steiner Collection.)

The famous Victory Club on North Clark Street, where Lee Collins played on and off for a dozen years, had a "For Rent" sign hanging when John Steiner shot this photograph c. 1968.

At left, Lee Collins is pictured at the Victory Club. The Victory was Collins' sometime-home for over 10 years. Collins recorded with his Astoria Eight, Jelly Roll Morton's Red Hot Peppers, as well as others. Sitting in with him on the piano is Little Brother Montgomery. (Photo by Richard Mushlitz.)

Pictured here at North Clark Street's Victory Club are two great New Orleans trumpeters: Lee Collins and his friend, Louis Armstrong. Lee Collins, in his fine book Oh Didn't He Ramble? *tells us a lot of history of the life of a musician. Through his eyes, we see the Great Migration from New Orleans to Chicago, where he states, "At one time Chicago looked like New Orleans." (Steiner Collection.)*

More often than not, Collins had the Victory Club to himself, blowing a solo for each instrument to everyone's amusement. However, on this 1951 job, Lee had a jam session going with Walter Morgan on trombone and Jeep Robinson on tenor sax. (Steiner Collection.)

Down the street from the Victory Club on North Clark Street was Frank O'Donnel's. O'Donnel's had an upstairs lounge where Lee Collins came to play for some extra cash. (Demlinger Photograph.)

Jack Gardner was a fine piano player. Gardner was not always sitting solo, as he played on several of Harry James' hit records. (Steiner Collection.)

North Wells Street was full of jazz clubs. Across the street from Franz Jackson's Dixieland group at the Old Town Gate was the Midas Touch as seen in this 1965 photo. Judy Roberts headlined a jazz group there and on Sundays, the club hosted jam sessions. (Demlinger Photograph.)

This photograph of jazz clarinetist Franz Jackson shows him listening to a tape of his bands. Jackson's Dixieland band played all over Chicago and in the 1960s, they were at the Old Town Gate when this night shot of Wells Street was taken. In the early recordings of jazz, the leading publishers and recorders were in Chicago simply because Chicago was the hub of music. Studios for Okeh, Paramount, QRS, Victor, Brunswick, Vocalion, Autograph, and Columbia were all in Chicago. Even the Gennett Studios were not far away in Richmond, Indiana. (Steiner Photograph.)

Along North Wells Street, every other store had music in it. Old Town Gate was the "House of Dixieland," as the sign reads. Franz Jackson and his All-Star Band was there for an extended period. The band was small, but featured a tuba player who shook the house down when he played. (Demlinger Photograph.)

Louis Armstrong cracks up over something said by his sidekicks Henry Red Allen, J.C. Higginbottom, and tenor man Ben Webster. (Steiner Collection.)

The Showboat *was docked along the Chicago River when John Steiner took this photograph. It was a dine and dance boat featuring swing and Dixieland. (Steiner Photograph.)*

On Chicago's Superior Street, this shot shows music greats, from left to right, Barrett Deems, drummer; Bud Freeman, tenor sax; Professor Ray Wilding White, organizer; John Barry, bass; and Jimmie McPartland, cornet; Art Hodes, piano, is seated in front. (Steiner Collection.)

Far right: This photograph with Albert Albee looking at the menu, shows Kelly's Stable on Chicago's Near North Side, named because the floor was covered with hay.

Immediate right: D.W. Griffith, the silent motion picture director, is quoted in this advertisement for Kelly's. (Chicago Jazz Archives / Steiner Collection.)

Below: Not far from Kelly's Stables on Rush, jazz lovers could find a lot going on up and down North Wells Street. This c. 1967 photo, below, shows a night street scene of Wells. (Demlinger Photograph.)

This close-up shot shows the Plugged Nickel, a little place on North Wells Street, which posted its coming attractions every week. Gloria Lynn was opening on this week's bill followed by the John Coltrane Quartet, Art Blakley and his Jazz Messengers, Sonny Stitt, Carmen McRae, Red Fox, Dizzy Gillespie, and more. The Plugged Nickel was the *place for be-bop. (Demlinger Photograph.)*

Here is the entire building that housed the Plugged Nickel, a Near North Side jazz house that featured the best talent anywhere. On the bill in this 1965 photograph were Sonny Stitt, Eddie Harris, and Roy Meriwether. (Demlinger Photograph.)

This action shot features an unidentified trombonist, Lee Collins on trumpet, and Darnell Howard on clarinet. (Steiner Collection.)

Doc Evans was an all-around horn man who played with jazz bands and symphonies. He had a brilliant brassy tone and no-nonsense phrasing. In large part through the promotion and encouragement of Dr. John Lucas of Winona, Minnesota, Doc came to Chicago in the 1950s when traditional jazz revival was at its height. He became the leader of bands that performed throughout the Midwest and recorded for five or six different labels.

Jimmy Granato, to whom the photograph is dedicated, was a longtime member of Doc's contingent. Jimmy sometimes worked as a leader, but more frequently he went into Art Hodes' groups after Doc retired in the late 1960s. Doc retired into the far northeast corner of Minnesota (Gran Marais), persuading pianist Frank Gillis to move to an adjacent property so the two could play together after Gillis retired as head of the University of Indiana's Traditional Jazz Archive. (Steiner Collection.)

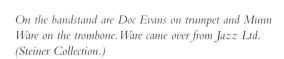

On the bandstand are Doc Evans on trumpet and Munn Ware on the trombone. Ware came over from Jazz Ltd. (Steiner Collection.)

Dave Garroway, far left, is the host of this radio jam session. The musicians include Marion McPartland on piano, Charlie Ventura on sax, Shelly Mann on drums, and Jimmy McPartland on the trumpet. (Steiner Collection.)

In 1940, the Gaffers Club on Wacker Drive featured live jazz. Pictured, from left to right, are Floyd O'Brien on trombone, Jag Burger on clarinet, Bill Tinker on trumpet, Boyce Brown on alto sax, Freddie Flynn on drums, and Tut Soper on piano. (Steiner Collection.)

Another jam session at the Gaffers Club on Wacker Drive features Bud Freeman on tenor sax, center. (Steiner Collection.)

The Liberty Inn is broadly advertised on the right side of its building on North Clark Street. A few doors south of the Liberty Inn was the Victory Club, which featured the hot trumpet of Lee Collins. Collins played at the Liberty off and on between 1930 and 1950. Long after Lee Collins was gone and the Victory Club closed, the Liberty Inn was still selling out nightly jam sessions, not with jazz but with Chuck and Sunny Bob and the Tenneseeians. This photograph was taken in 1963. The area has since been replaced with a parking lot. (Demlinger Photograph.)

This photo shows the close quarters of the Jazz Ltd. bandstand on Grand Avenue. Owner Bill Reinhardt is playing clarinet on the left with Big Sid Catlett on drums and Joe Sullivan on piano. (Steiner Collection.)

At right: This insert from Down Beat heralds Sidney Bechet's first appearance in Chicago since 1918, which was at Jazz Ltd.

Here is a rare and early photograph of North Howard Street taken from the El tracks facing east. On the left side of the street is the city of Evanston, Illinois, which did not allow liquor to be sold within its city limits. The Howard Café, later called the Lime House, featured weekend dance bands well into the late 1950s. Along this street, jazz clubs such as the Bandbox and Club Silhouette featured great musicians such as Charlie Ventura. (Demlinger Collection.)

CHAPTER SIX

North Side

1920s–1960s

THE NORTH SIDE OF CHICAGO is an area filled with distinct neighborhoods. This chapter will touch upon the area of the city from Howard Street on the north, the Lake on the east, and Fullerton Avenue on the south.

Just north of the city limits, Evanston was a dry town. People living there who were looking for a night on the town, complete with alcoholic beverages, had to travel to Chicago, and Howard Street was the closest spot. As early as the 1920s, there was much to see and do on this street. Lined with theaters, bars, saloons, restaurants, and other places that catered to patrons, college students, and anyone out for a good time, Howard Street and Rogers Park had a lot to offer the jazz scene.

The large Howard Theater had stage acts, vaudeville shows, and movies. It had a large pit band like the major theaters of downtown. As Northwestern University was not far from Howard Street many students would come on weekend breaks or on holidays. Most of the bars and saloons had some form of music going on during the weekends.

During World War II, every place was open to the Army's Fort Sheridan soldiers and the Great Lakes Training Station sailors. After the war, Howard Street was still home to many top music and jazz clubs.

The Casa Bonita had a Dixieland band led by trumpeter Doc Evans. The Club Silhouette was the hot club on the strip featuring talent from the full orchestra of Woody Herman's Herd to singer Nellie Letcher and her trio. Then, in the 1950s, Louis Armstrong's great All-Star Band, which consisted of Sid Catlett on drums, Jack Teagarden on trombone, and Barney Bigard on clarinet performed at the Club Silhouette for a prolonged stay. This place was a hit. Louis and Teagarden sang duets from many of their memorable recorded hits; the crowd loved it. When I finally caught up with them, they had moved to the Rag Doll Lounge on north Western Avenue. Every jazz great played at the Club Silhouette and when Louis left, in came Dizzy Gillespie and his be-bop band.

Only a few doors away stood the Bandbox, where Charlie Ventura and his combo held down the fort and sometimes had drummer Gene Krupa sit in. Krupa featured Ventura on tenor on many recordings for his band. Ventura was usually playing clubs all over the city, but it seemed the Bandbox was his home.

A few blocks south of Howard on Thorndale Street you could find Rupnecks Lounge. There Danny Alvin would sit at his drums and lead his Dixieland band on any famous song from the 1920s. If Danny had gone off for a few weeks, Art Hodes would replace him on the piano, leading another Dixieland band. They would often play the Normandy Lounge or Rupnecks lounge, whichever needed them.

Sometimes George Brunies would leave his sure thing at the 1111 Club on Bryn Mawr near the El station and venture out to Skokie, a northern suburb of Chicago. There at the Club Down Beat on Dempster Avenue, he would treat the fans to some real down to earth singing and playing— New Orleans style. Brunies had a great lineup to play with at the 1111 Club. There was a toothless Hey Hey Humphries on drums and Johnny Lane or Doc Evans on trumpet; these guys could knock your shoes off. When Brunies would finish his fifth chorus or so and the people applauded, he would shy them off and pantomime them to drink up by lifting his cupped hand to his lips. I had the chance to talk to Brunies one evening. At the time, he was trying to get some people interested in organizing an old musicians' home, much like they do for Hollywood's retired actors. But he never did pull that off, though it would have been great. The last time I talked to him he was catching a typical Chicago flu. When Brunies left the stand at the 1111 Club, Muggsy Spanier took over the lead and brought in a piano player named Roy Wasson, who sounded a lot like Jelly Roll Morton.

Many of the larger hotels on Chicago's North Side held dances and had large indoor and outdoor ballrooms. The famous Edgewater Beach Hotel held some spectacular dances. Outside, on their large dance floor, they would contract the best bands of the time. A long lighted gangway led from the ballroom to the lake and made for a romantic evening as couples could walk and dance under the stars. At the large Gramere Hotel, also along Sheridan Road, there was a large ballroom that featured the usual sweet bands, but sometimes they would book top swing orchestras like Tommy or Jimmy Dorsey's Orchestra.

Not far from all this was the North Side's leading dance ballroom, the Aragon Ballroom, which is still on Lawrence Avenue in Uptown. When it opened, the Aragon booked every large dance orchestra that came to town. The ballroom's setting was like that of a European palace, complete with an ornate interior and painted stars and ceiling lights.

Just down the street, on Lawrence and Broadway, is one of Chicago's landmark music establishments, the Green Mill Lounge. However, it was originally up the stairs and was called the Green Mill Gardens. The Green Mill remains today and features outstanding music for listening and dancing.

A few doors away stands the large Uptown Theater, which in earlier days had stage shows and vaudeville performers plus the movie hits of the day. Across the street is another large theater called the Riveria. The Terminal and Metro across the street were great neighborhood movie houses, and around the corner was a small artist theater called the Alba. Farther north was the giant Granada Theater, which had some of the country's largest and best sweet orchestras on its stage.

Farther west on the North Side was Chicago's Riverview Park, which featured an outside ballroom lit by hundreds of small colored lights for summer dancers. Long before any jazz music was heard around Chicago, the Riverview Park dance pavilion was a paradise for many. It was torn down to make room for a shopping center.

Just north of Chicago is an outdoor concert pavilion known as Ravinia. Normally home to opera and classical music, in August of 1938 it was turned into swing heaven. With a crowd estimated at over 8,500, much more than the limited seating could hold, the Benny Goodman Orchestra was at the top of their form. Goodman, Teddy Wilson, Lionel Hampton, and Dave Tough, with Harry James also in the band, delighted the crowd. It was the kind of musical explosion that only a band like this could produce.

The North Side of Chicago, from the edge of town and beyond, was ripe with jazz music, swinging orchestras, hip hotels, and beautiful ballrooms. Today, each North Side neighborhood offers something a little different, all the while affected by the flavor of its history.

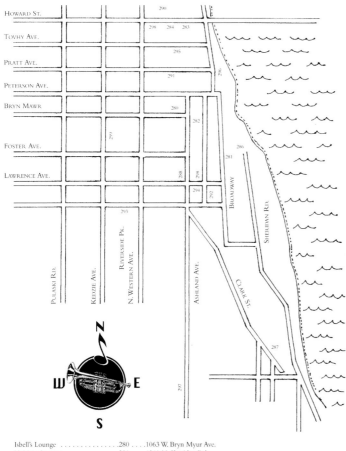

NORTH SIDE

Isbell's Lounge . . . . .280 . . . .1063 W. Bryn Myur Ave.
Heisings Lounge . . . . .281 . . . .4361 N. Sheridan Rd.
1111 Club . . . . .282 . . . .El Train @ Bryn Myur Ave
Lime House Restaurant . . . . .283 . . . .E. Howard St. Near El Train
Club Silhouette . . . . .284 . . . .Howard St.
Gramere Hotel 285
Edge Water Beach Hotel . . . . . . .286 . . . .N. Sheridan Rd. & Foster Ave.
El-Royals (Ballroom) . . . . .288 . . . .443 N. Clark St.
Rainbow Gardens (Ballroom) . . . .288 . . . .N. Clark St. at Lawrence Ave.
The Green Mill . . . . .289 . . . .N. Broadway and Lawrence Ave.
Ravinia (Outdoor Music Bowl) . . .290 . . . .North Suburbs
Normandy Lounge 291
Aragon Ball Room . . . . .292 . . . .Lawrence Ave. at El Stop
Riverview Park . . . . .293 . . . .N. Western Ave. & Addison Ave.
Montmarte Cafe . . . . .294 . . . .Broadway at Lawrence Ave.
Rupneck's Lounge . . . . .295 . . . .1127 Thorndale Ave.
Granada Theater . . . . .296 . . . .Sheridan Ave.
John Steiner's house . . . . .297 . . . .N. Greenview St. (Early) N. Ashland Ave.
The Band Box . . . . .298 . . . .Howard St. at El Train
The Rag Doll Club . . . . .299 . . . .N. Western Ave.
Uptown Theater . . . . .300 . . . .Broadway Ave. & Lawrence Ave.

In 1949, the Club Silhouette held an informal reunion of Chicago musicians. Pictured here, from left to right, are the following: Brad Gowans (piano); front row (kneeling): John Schenck , Doc Evans, Tony Parenti, Wild Bill Davidson, Chet Roble, Johnny Lane, Lee Collins, and Freddie Flynn; (standing) Brownie McGee, Danny Alvin, Miff Mole, Doc Cenardo, Jimmie James, Bill Pfeiffer, Bill Tinkler, Herb Ward, and Mama Yancey; (back row) Bud Jacobson, Art Hodes, and Jimmy Yancey. (Steiner Collection.)

Doctor Jazz on West Wilson Avenue featured small combos. Headliners included Jack the Bear and Browns Band. (Steiner Collection.)

A collage of show club business cards includes among them the Club Silhouette on Howard Street on the North Side, which featured Louis Armstrong's All-Stars with Big Sid Catlett on drums, Barney Biogard on clarinet, Jack Teagarden on trombone, Earl Hines on piano, and Velma Middleton on vocals. (Steiner Collection.)

In the late 1950s, the Rag Doll Lounge had a great week hosting Louis Armstrong and the Esquire All-Stars. The group, pictured here from left to right, was Big Sid Catlett on drums, Barney Bigard on clarinet, Louis Armstrong on trumpet, Earl Hines at the piano, Jack Teagarden on trombone, and Arvell Shaw on bass. (Steiner Collection.)

At right: Chicago had many fine restaurants featuring music on the North Side. Rupnecks at 1127 West Thorndale was one such place, seen here in 1949. With headliner Danny Alvin on drums, the other members are, from left to right, Johnny Lane, Bill Tinker, Art Gromwell, and Jimmy James. (Steiner Collection.)

Pictured above is a truly great ensemble of players led by Jimmy McPartland. They are, from left to right, Joe Sullivan on piano, George Brunies on trombone, Jimmy McPartland on trumpet, Eddie Condon on guitar, and Pee Wee Russell on clarinet. (Steiner Collection.)

At right: Although the Casa Loma Orchestra traveled around the country, it often played at Chicago's larger hotels in the 1920s and 1930s. (Steiner Collection.)

The Green Mill, a Chicago landmark for jazz in the 1920s, was originally called the Green Mill Gardens. Its ballroom was upstairs from the present street-level Green Mill Club. The stone-engraved sign is still there. (Demlinger Photograph.)

MAIN DINING ROOM

Montmartre Cafe

I. Bookshester and Bob Strauss, *Props.*

"Chicago's Most Interesting Amusement Place"

Entertainment That's Refined — Yet Snappy

Highest Paid Entertainers in Chicago

Vaudeville Headliner

Jules Buffano and His Sensational Dance Orchestra

SEVEN COURSE—Table D'Hote D

ALSO

A la Carte Serv

"BEST STEAK IN

MONTMARTR

Broadway at Lawrence

The North Side's Montmartre Cafe, at Broadway and Lawrence, featured vaudeville acts plus some good music. The location is very close to the still-operating Green Mill Lounge, and the Aragon Ballroom. Paul Zimms and his Chicagoans played the Montmartre off and on for quite some time. (Steiner Collection.)

At right: A great lineup of Dixieland stars play one of their favorites. Pictured here, from left to right; are Jimmie Noone on clarinet, Joe Sullivan on piano, Johnny Lane on trumpet, Miff Mole on trombone, and Baby Dodds on drums. (Steiner Collection.)

The Rainbow Gardens on North Clark Street and Lawrence Avenue featured the orchestra of Isham Jones. The building was turned into a roller rink and then back to a dance ballroom that featured the major big bands playing songs from the 1940s and 1950s. (Demlinger Collection.)

Pictured is the interior of the above Rainbow Garden Ballroom. The ballroom had live radio broadcasts playing music. (Demlinger Collection.)

Pictured here is the Aragon Ballroom on near North Broadway and Lawrence Avenue. Its lush interiors and headliner orchestras made a night out on their dance floor very exciting. As of 2003, the Aragon was still operating as a Chicago music venue. (Demlinger Photograph.)

This October 8, 1938 Aragon Ballroom publication advertises an upcoming performance by "Benny Goodman and the World's Greatest Swing Band."

A jam session in Chicago wouldn't be complete without some of the real pioneers pictured here: Baby Dodds on drums; Bud Freeman on sax; and Muggsy Spanier on trumpet. (Don Erman.)

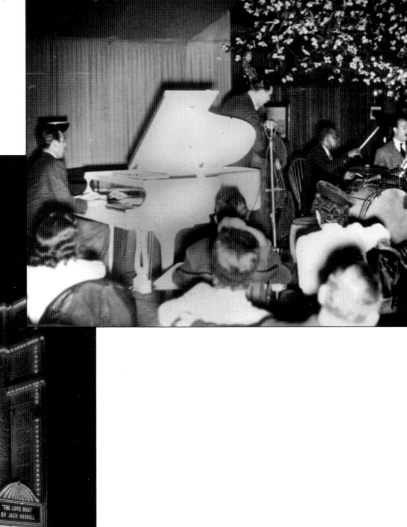

The North Side's elegant Granada Theater drew crowds with Benny Meroff's orchestra, which featured the trumpet of Wild Bill Davis. This glass-plate print was made in 1926 by Kaufmann & Fabry. (Demlinger Collection.)

The 1111 Club on Bryn Mawr was home to George Brunies for many years. He played here with many talented musicians over the years. (Chuck Senstock.)

This is a 1942 photograph of Art Hodes' birthday party. Many of his pals came out to celebrate, including Jimmy Yancey, Hey Hey Humphries, Down Beat writer George Hoefer, Miff Mole, and Mama Yancey. Hodes is in the center. (Steiner Collection.)

At the Normandy Show Lounge on Chicago's North Side, a good time was had by all, including Jimmy Granato on the clarinet, Doc Evans on trumpet, Miff Mole on trombone, and Art Hodes on the piano. Hodes played along with his own band at the Normandy for a long time. One could walk up the street to the 1111 Club and get a year's worth of great trombone by George Brunies in an hour. (Steiner Collection.)

It was a hot summer day in 1938 when Benny Goodman took his orchestra to Ravinia Park to play for 8,500 swing lovers. On August 4, 1938, the Chicago Daily Times reported that Goodman gave the listeners a swinging treat. In this photograph, Benny's back-ups include Teddy Wilson on the piano, Dave Tough on drums, and Lionel Hampton on vibes. (Steiner Collection.)

"Jammin' at John's" (John Steiner) could be the title of this fine photograph by Ward Silver showing Woody Senerling on violin, Tut Soper on the piano, and Bill Preutty on guitar.

Don Ewell follows a score while playing piano at John Steiner's house. (Steiner Photograph.)

Above: Ward Silver gives us a nice close-up photograph of Tut Super playing those keys.

Above: With his trumpet in hand, Jimmy McPartland clowns it up for guitarist Les Paul. (Steiner Collection.)

At right: Boyce Brown gets in his licks while fellow jazzman Muggsy Spanier backs him up. (Steiner Collection.)

Above: Early in his career, Duke Ellington posed for this fine portrait in the Bloom Studios of Chicago. (Demlinger Collection.)

Dizzy Gillespie and his small group blow up a storm during this one-nighter. (Demlinger Photograph.)

CHAPTER SEVEN

West Side

1920s–1969

MUCH LIKE THE OTHER areas in Chicago, the West Side was home to distinct neighborhoods. As early as 1910, the streets of the city marked off the ethnic areas and separated the races. Pulaski Road (Crawford Avenue) was a so-called boundary line, as were Central and Harlem Avenues. The diversity that made Chicago a city of neighborhoods was evident on the West Side, which hosted Germans, Irish, Italian, and Jewish enclaves.

Chicago's West Side was home to a great many beer halls complete with entertainers performing almost every weekend and even during the week. If the halls were not beer halls, they were athletic clubs that served beer. Here, dances would be held every weekend, sometimes starting on Friday, with parties continuing until Sunday night.

Some of these halls included Hoerber's Hall on Blue Island Avenue and Schoenhofen's Hall at Milwaukee and Ashland Avenues. There was the Bender's Athletic and Benevolent Association at the Northwest Club, Lauterbach's Hall, which featured music by Cook's Union Orchestra, and even the Yorkshire Rod and Gun Association held annual dances. The Gaelic Athletic Association held an Annual Irish Ball with music by Curran and O'Hara's Orchestra. Angler's Benevolent Association held an annual benefit at Vorwaert's Turner Hall that featured Otto Blazek and his orchestra playing two-step music.

While the area was teeming with music, from the outside looking in it seemed there was very little jazz music being played at these events. It seems almost a miracle that the bunch from Austin High got together at all. This bunch produced an amazing group of musicians and influenced the work of many others. From Benny Goodman, Jimmy McPartland, PeeWee Russell, and Frankie Teschmaker, to George Wettling, Dave Tough, Eddie Condon, Joe Sullivan, and Gene Krupa, to name a few, the group made its mark. The kids from the West Side found out what was

happening on the city's South Side and got ahold of the recordings of King Joe Oliver, Jelly Roll Morton, and Louis Armstrong. When they found out that these guys were right there in the city, you couldn't keep them away.

The aforementioned musicians worked after school to pay for their instruments. They took weekend jobs playing at dances, parties, and beer halls. On Garfield Boulevard by the El train stop was the Golden Lily Supper Club. There, bands like Sam Wamby's would play during the dinner hours. But after hours, the Austin High gang received the managements "okay" to get up on stage and do their razz-ma-taz hot jazz.

Important to the West Side's development of jazz music, especially in the Chicago style, was Hull House. While Benny Goodman's name was associated with this school and place, a lot of other musicians learned to play their instruments there during their youth as well.

While the West Side's Austin High gang leaned heavily in favor of the New Orleans' sounds they heard on the South Side, they also picked up ideas and music from some of the early white musicians. The style they came away with was neither that of New Orleans or Dixieland, but their own rough sounding music, which later came to be known as Chicago Style. Soon, some of the young leaders were fronting their own bands.

Jimmy McPartland was leading the way on cornet at the White City Ballroom on 63rd Street. They called themselves Husk O'Hare's Wolverines. This band included Frank Teschmaker on clarinet, Bud Freeman on alto and tenor, Dick McPartland, Dave Tough, Floyd O'Brien, and Jim Lanigan. Joe Sullivan would sit in on the piano with the group on weekends.

The musicians who came from the city's West Side have had a resounding affect on the city's jazz music scene. Their distinct style, particular to Chicago, has helped to define the local jazz scene.

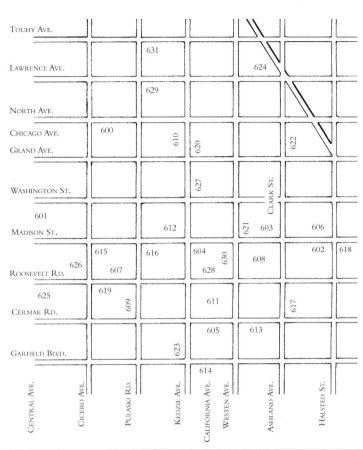

WEST SIDE

A nearly deserted Polk Street is seen here in 1915. (Demlinger Collection.)

Frankie Trumbauer fronts his orchestra in this 1932 photograph. Pictured, from left to right, are the following: (front row) Leon "Krappy" Kaplan, guitar; Cedric Spring, violin; unidentified; Trumbauer, leader and alto sax; Gale Stout, tenor sax; Mac Elstad, clarinet; and Harold Jones, tenor; (back row) Herman Crone, piano; Charles McConell, bass; Hal Reders, vocalist; Leroy Buck, drums and vocal; Max Connett, trumpet; Max Chink Rice, manager and trumpet; and Hal Matthews, trombone. (Steiner Collection.)

Many future jazz musicians passed through this entrance on their way to classes at the famous Austin High School on the West Side. (Steiner Collection.)

Jimmy McPartland listens to the tape that he and the other musicians had just made at Steiner's. (Steiner Photograph.)

Pictured is the rejuvenated Hull House on the campus of the University of Illinois at Chicago. It was here that Benny Goodman and many other children had the opportunity to take music instruction. (Demlinger Photograph.)

At right: Chicagoan Eddie Condon sits on a barstool with pal Joe Sullivan on his right, talking to a fan. (Steiner Photograph.)

Below, right: In this photo, Jimmy McPartland, on trombone, steps to the microphone to play a few choruses. (Photo from Mr. and Mrs. Frank J. Gillis.)

Below, left: This early photograph shows Chicago drum master Gene Krupa in the early days of Benny Goodman's band. (Steiner Collection.)

RAY MILLER AND HIS BRUNSWICK ORCHESTRA

Ray Miller's Orchestra is seen here in a Brunswick Recording Company publicity photograph. The orchestra played all over Chicago, often at Chicago's major hotels. (Chicago Jazz Archives/Steiner Collection.)

A radio show called Jam and Jive *was broadcast locally. The legends pictured in this rare photograph are, from left to right, Baby Dodds on drums, Natty Dominique on trumpet, Johnny Dodds on clarinet, unknown bass player and guitarist, and Lil Armstrong on the piano. (Steiner Collection.)*

Gene Krupa and his orchestra pose for a formal portrait. In this photograph, Gene is behind the drums, Vido Musso is in the sax section, and Anita Oday is the vocalist. (Steiner Collection.)

OPPOSITE: *On the bandstand is a girl harpist who played in drummer Dave Tough's small band at a West Side club. (Steiner Photograph.)*

This young group of college students was called the Cake Walking Babies. This 1948 action shot includes Ted Bielefeld on soprano sax, Birch Smith on cornet, and Jeff Cearnt. (Steiner Photograph.)

The Salty Dogs are seen here at the Red Arrow Lounge at 6927 Pershing Road in 1952 playing their Dixieland-style jazz. Pictured here, from left to right, are Jerry Jordan on drums, Amrand Vandr Heydt on clarinet, John Ely on trumpet, Otto Kunkel's (grandson) Kazon, Don Ewell on piano, Ralph Mason on trombone, and Dick Mushlitz on banjo. (From Dick Mushlitz.)

Above: For a decade in the middle of the century, pianist Dick Marx and bassman Johnny Frigo dominated the scene as informal accompanists. Marx went into writing and directing commercial ditties, and Frigo found his greatest appreciation as Chicago's prime hot fiddler. (Steiner Collection.)

At right: It looks like these happy four just came from a parade. Holding the cornet is Sid Dawson. (Duncan Schiedt Collection.)

This is a rare, early photograph of the Crane Tech High School band class. Although not as famous as the bands at DuSable and Wendell Phillips High Schools, it turned out very capable musicians. (Steiner Collection.)

Pictured here are some interesting sheet music with bands and orchestras on the covers. Pictured on the cover of the "Wolverine Blues" is the famous New Orleans Rhythm Kings, who played at the Friar's Club. This group included George Brunies on trombone who played around Chicago for most of his life. Most of these bands on the sheet music covers appeared at Chicago hotels and ballrooms. (Steiner Collection.)

A photo of the Original Dixieland Jazz Band was used on the cover of this sheet music of "Bluin' the Blues." The photograph on the cover includes Larry Shields and Nick Larocca, but it was actually the recordings of Muggsy Spanier and George Brunies that made this tune a favorite for years. (Steiner Collection.)

THE LATEST JAZZ SONG CRAZE

BLUIN' THE BLUES

LAROCCA   RAGAS

EDWARDS   SBARBARO   SHIELDS

ORIGINAL DIXIELAND JAZZ BAND

WORDS BY
SIDNEY D. MITCHELL

MUSIC BY
H.W. RAGAS
OF THE ORIGINAL
DIXIELAND JAZZ BAND

STANDARD LEO. FEIST INC. EDITION NEW YORK

James Kriegsmann took this great photograph of Muggsy Spanier. (Frank Gillis Collection.)

Metronome

MODERN MUSIC AND ITS MAKERS

BIX BEIDERBECKE

Bix Beiderbecke is seen here on the cover of a 1938 issue of Metronome. (Steiner Collection.)

157

Among West Madison Street's night spots in the 1930s and 1940s was the Mardi Gras. It later became a strip joint, but for a while it had live music for dancers. The sign of "All-Star Revues" usually meant an emcee with some filthy jokes before the star came floating out on stage. (Demlinger Photograph.)

The L&L Café on West Madison Street had all-girl revues during the war years and small bands playing for dancers. In the early 1950s, it featured stage revues and strippers. This photo was taken in 1965. (Demlinger Photograph.)

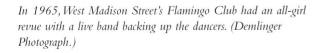

In 1965, West Madison Street's Flamingo Club had an all-girl revue with a live band backing up the dancers. (Demlinger Photograph.)

This interior shot of Cohen's Tavern, taken in 1960, catches a patron turning to see the camera, wondering if his photograph is being taken. (Demlinger Photograph.)

Pictured is the interior of a typical dine and dance establishment in the early 1930s. (Demlinger Collection.)

Chicago's West Side had large dancehalls in the 1930s. This photograph shows the Dreamland Ballroom on Van Buren Street. It has since been demolished. (Steiner Collection.)

This 1927 shot of the Marbro Theater promises a night of Tom Brown and his Original Six on stage. Brown, who played trombone, brought the first white New Orleans jazz band to Chicago in 1915. (Demlinger Collection.)

West Madison Street in 1920 was home to a place called Driscoll's Dreamland Ballroom, which hosted orchestras, including Pinky Cersette as leader and clarinetist, as well as bands, including Jack Schwartz. In later years, it became a bowling alley. (Steiner Collection.)

IT WAS APRIL 19, 1969, when John Steiner called me and told me to grab my 35-millimeter camera because he was picking me up to go with him to WTTW Channel 11, Chicago's educational television station. Performing that night were some true jazz music masters. It was a staged concert that had Coleman Hawkins on tenor sax and his best buddy Roy Eldridge on trumpet, with Barry Harris on piano, Truck Parham on bass, and drummer Bob Cousins keeping the beat.

With my trusted old Leica camera, I recorded the scene, taking what would be my last pictures for this jazz book and the last shots I took in Chicago for over 25 years. Hawkins dragged his tired body ever so slowly up to the stage and sat down. With a long gray beard, looking like a man from another time, he wore the snappy suit and shining shoes that illustrated the elegant person he was. The Hawk never missed a note through the entire set, which lasted almost 30 minutes. The small select crowd gave them a standing ovation after the set.

Hawkins was 65 years old, give or take another 20 years considering the fact that he led a musician's life. He passed away a month after this final taping of his music. A day later they played again at the North Park Hotel's Terrace Room, which was located on Clark and Armitage Avenues. The session was produced by the Chicago Jazz Institute and was their last jam session.

As jobs around Chicago began to dry up, many of the musicians traveled east to New York City where they were met with open arms. Leaders like Goodman and Krupa started their own large bands. With the arrangements of Fletcher Henderson to lean on, Goodman's group really made strides in the music industry. He attracted many great musical talents and soon his band was one big all-star group—with Bunny Berigen on trumpet and Jess Stacy on piano, not to mention leading trumpeters Harry James and Ziggy Elman. He also lined up Gene Krupa on drums and the gifted musician Lionel Hampton on vibes. But in one way or another, many of the West Side's young talents became leaders of their own bands. They bended with the wind, but they didn't break.

The following is a series of photographs from the Channel 11 broadcast. At right, Roy Eldridge plays trumpet with Truck Parham on string bass. (Demlinger Photograph.)

Above, Bob Cousins gets into his drum solo. (Demlinger Photograph.)

JAZZ INSTITUTE OF CHICAGO PROUDLY PRESENTS
— In Person —

All Ages Welcome

THE KING OF THE TENOR SAX
COLEMAN HAWKINS
TRUMPET GREAT — "LITTLE JAZZ"
ROY ELDRIDGE
— with —

Student ID Discount

BARRY HARRIS — Piano
FRANZ JACKSON'S SWINGTET

PARK TERRACE ROOM NORTH PARK HOTEL
1931 Lincoln Pk. West At Clark & Armitage

SUN. APRIL 20 • ONLY
(4 — 9 PM)

The day after the WTTW broadcast, the Jazz Institute of Chicago presented Coleman Hawkins, Roy Eldridge, Barry Harris, and Franz Jackson's Swingtet. (Demlinger Collection.)

Below: This shot shows Roy Eldridge at the height of his popularity. His musical accomplishments span many decades. (Demlinger Photograph.)

Above: Roy Eldridge takes a quick break while Truck Parham continues to jam on the string bass. (Demlinger Photograph.)

Tonight at 8

A television epitaph for Coleman Hawkins

By Tony Gieske

If you've already seen "Oh! Calcutta" and "I Am Curious (Yellow)," then Tuesday you can break the last great American taboo. You can watch a man actually dying — I don't mean like in a Western, I mean really dying — right in your very home, in living color.

The man was Coleman Hawkins, who died at the age of 65, on May 19, a month to the day after taping a half-hour show for WTTW (Ch. 11) here in Chicago, his last recorded performance. It will be shown Tuesday night at 8 p.m.

point: "He was first-class" and that, my friend, is the true facts.

ON THIS program — the original Hawkins tape is sandwiched between another half-hour of matter-of-fact, non-maudlin tribute — Eldridge says what he means by that is that when Hawkins bought a camera it was an M-3 Leica; a car, a Cadillac; a suit, $300, I think he meant something else, too, like these jazz guys often do.

Hawkins plays most of the show seated, the patient bones literally showing through his $300 suit, his body utterly immobile when he is not performing.

Jefferson to Hawkins' most famous solo, "Body and Soul."

IT IS difficult to write of Hawkins' performance. That born was his life, and you can hear it getting away from him, and you know that he knows it. He can hear what he wants to play in his head, you are sure, but the fingers won't cooperate. So he keeps it very, very simple and very, very pure. In a half-hour, I heard him miss just one note.

With him — and I mean really with him — are Barry Harris, piano; Truck Parham, bass, and Bob Cousins, drums. For the later segments, they are joined by Franz Jackson,

COLEMAN HAWKINS
A pro to the end

Coleman Hawkins, tenor sax, and Barry Harris, piano, are seen at the Channel 11 broadcast above. (Demlinger Photograph.)

Coleman passed away on May 19, 1969, exactly one month after the taping of the WTTW program. (Demlinger Collection.)

Pianist Barry Harris entertains tenor man Coleman Hawkins. (Demlinger Photograph.)

This action shot of the WTTW recording shows Truck Parham on bass, Roy Eldridge on trumpet, and Bob Cousins on the drums. (Demlinger Photograph.)

THE LEGENDS OF CHICAGO JAZZ have made a lasting and profound affect on the musical landscape. Their musical style has helped to define a distinctly American form that has influenced so much more than music. This collection of photos, while by no means a comprehensive history of Chicago jazz, is intended as an homage to the great men and women who shaped this important aspect of Chicago history.